Everything You Need to Know About Creative Writing

Also available from Continuum

Teaching Creative Writing edited by Graeme Harper
The Creative Writing MFA Handbook by Tom Kealey

Everything You Need to Know About

CREATIVE WRITING

(but knowing isn't everything . . .)

Heather Leach and Robert Graham

continuum

Continuum

The Tower Building, 11 York Road, London SE1 7NX
80 Maiden Lane, Suite 704, New York NY 10038

www.continuumbooks.com

British Library Cataloguing-in-Publication Data
A catalogue record for this book is available from the British Library.

ISBN: 0-8264-9021-2 (hardback)
    978-0-8264-9021-6
    0-8264-9022-0 (paperback)
    978-0-8264-9022-3

Library of Congress Cataloging-in-Publication Data
A catalog record for this book is available from the Library of Congress.

Typeset by Kenneth Burnley, Wirral, Cheshire
Printed and bound in Great Britain by MPG Books Ltd, Bodmin, Cornwall

Contents

Contributors   vii

Introduction   1

Abstract to Zeitgeist   **3–190**

Further Reading and Useful Websites   191

Alternative Routes   193

Contributors

Heather Leach for many years taught Creative Writing at Manchester Metropolitan University. Her short fiction and non-fiction work has appeared in a variety of media including *The Big Issue* and BBC Radio and she won the *Times Higher Education Supplement* Essay Competition in 2004. She is co-editor of *The Road to Somewhere: A Creative Writing Companion* (Palgrave, 2005) and is currently involved in a collaborative writing project with the University of Lleida in Spain.

Robert Graham teaches Creative Writing at Manchester Metropolitan University, Cheshire. His short stories have appeared in magazines and anthologies and on BBC Radio 4. His novel, *Holy Joe*, was published by Troubador in 2006. He is the co-author, with Keith Baty, of *Elvis – The Novel* (The Do-Not Press, 1997). He is co-author and co-editor of *The Road To Somewhere: A Creative Writing Companion* (Palgrave, 2005) and author of *How To Write Fiction (And Think About It)* (Palgrave, 2006).

Contributors

Gareth Creer runs Free To Write, a project which works with inmates and ex-offenders. He lectures in Imaginative Writing at Liverpool John Moores University and his novels, *Skin and Bone*, *Cradle To Grave* and *Big Sky*, are published by Transworld and in translation. He has also written for the *New Statesman*, *Sunday Times* and *Daily Telegraph*. His short fiction has been published by *Penguin*, *City Life*, *Headland* and *Waterside*.

Ursula Hurley teaches Creative Writing at the University of Salford. She has published poetry, articles and short stories widely and is currently working on a novel as part of her PhD thesis.

Helen Newall is the Programme Leader for the Drama, Physical Theatre and Dance degree at Edge Hill University. She has written plays for the Nuffield Theatre, Southampton. She was writer in residence at the Chester Gateway Theatre. Her short fiction has appeared in *Myslexia*, *Pool* and *Pretext*. She is co-editor of *The Road to Somewhere: A Creative Writing Companion* (Palgrave, 2005).

Jenny Newman is a Reader in Creative Writing at Liverpool John Moores University. She has published two novels, *Going In* (Penguin, 1994) and *Life Class* (Arrow, 2000). She is a contributing co-editor of *The Writer's Workbook* (Arnold, 2004) and of *British and Irish Novelists: An Introduction Through Interviews* (Arnold, 2004). Her short fiction has appeared in *The London Magazine* and on BBC Radio 4.

Harriet Tarlo is Programme Manager for Creative Writing at the University of Leeds. Her poetry publications include *Love/Land* (Rem Press, 2003), NAB (etruscan books, 2005), *Poems 1990–2003* (Shearsman, 2004), as well as appearances in anthologies and magazines. She has published critical essays on modernist and contemporary poetry in journals such as *Sagetrieb*, *Feminist Review* and *How2* and her books have been published by Edinburgh University Press, Rodopi and Macmillan.

Introduction

This book is an alphabetical guide to creative writing, intended to provide a clear, accessible and readable overview for student writers and their tutors. We hope that you will find it informative and stretching, a guide that you can use for quick reference, but which will also draw you into a deeper exploration of craft, theory and practice. It offers definitions of key terms, advice on creative process and publishing, practical writing exercises, comment on theoretical, cultural and political issues, as well as guidance for further research. We have also tried to include the occasional flash of lightness and humour.

Entries range from the briefest definition to the short essay. Some discuss familiar topics, such as plot, character, dialogue and rhyme, while others explore less well-known terms such as voice, transition and phoneme. There are generic entries – for example, autobiography, poetry, fiction, monologue, scriptwriting and the short story. There are entries that relate to the writer's life (block, desk, reading, publication and workshops), while others touch on broader issues, gender, language, political correctness, race – but examined from a Creative Writing perspective. There are also entries on experimental, off-the-page and interactive writing practices such as blogs, e-books, graphic novels, metafiction and performance. Most entries include practical writing ideas and longer entries also have suggestions for further reading and practice.

As well as the basic A–Z structure, there are 'Alternative Routes' lists at the back of the book, which bring together related entries. These focused lists can be used by individual students to explore a particular topic, or by tutors planning a lesson or longer programme of study. The entries and alternative routes can also help student writers undertaking academic study to reflect on their creative practice.

This book is optimistically entitled *Everything You Need to Know About Creative Writing*, but we are very well aware that such a claim, however larkily tongue-in-cheek, is doomed to fall short. We have tried to be as comprehensive as possible and to include the key elements that make up the

Introduction

Creative Writing field. We have selected topics we consider important, based on our experience as writers and writing teachers, and have drawn on a range of distinguished contributors, but there are bound to be important subjects we have missed out. We are also aware, as our subtitle indicates, that a great deal of what goes on in any creative practice depends on other kinds of knowledge, and on different ways of using texts and language than are usually explored within conventional academic guides and pedagogical discourses. We hope that any omissions will stimulate you to fill in the gaps for yourselves, and that you will also be able to follow the faint traces of those other forms of knowledge and language that are indicated here.

There are many ways to use this book: you can dip in and out; you can jump interactively from one entry to another using the many cross-references; you can follow one of the alternative routes to explore a specific topic in more detail; you can try out the writing ideas; and use the reading suggestions to go further and deeper. We hope that you will find it a practical, creative and thought-provoking guide.

Heather Leach and Robert Graham

abstract

Abstract words describe feelings, emotions, ideas or generalizations: *socialism, fear, sadness, hate, religion, hope* are all abstractions. If in doubt about whether a word is abstract, try the imaginary sense-test. Could it be touched, smelt, tasted, seen, heard? If not, it's abstract. You can directly experience a kiss or a slap but not love or anger. All writing is a mix of both abstract and concrete language but huge emotional words like *hope, hate* and *suffering* can distance both writer and reader from genuine feeling. Semi-abstract generalizations like *fruit, bird, colour*, etc., create only vague pictures in the mind. Better to use *tangerine, pigeon, yellow*.   *HL*

(See **concrete**)

action

What characters do. The function of characters in fiction and scriptwriting is twofold: action (what they do) and dialogue (what they say). Fiction that doesn't work often suffers from insufficient action. A static plot, for instance, will kill any story. Readers like to see proactive protagonists who are a little larger than life, so it isn't just any old action that will do, but action that leans towards the heroic. Ideally, your understanding of your characters will dictate what they do. Characters can't help but behave characteristically, so be sure that the action you decide on is what this character would do.   *RG*

adjective

A word which adds a feature or quality to a noun or pronoun, sometimes called a describing word. Adjectives can be used before the noun, as in: a *yellow* car; a *sharp* knife; or after the verb, as in: he was *thin*, the cat was *black*. Use adjectives with precision to give depth, colour and texture to your writing.   *HL*

(See **concrete**)

advance

The sum of money paid to an author in advance of any sales received by the publisher. This is seldom paid in advance of the book having been written, though sometimes a publisher will negotiate an advance for a series of books (i.e. if they like your first book they may give you a two-book deal to secure your follow-up).

A commonly held myth is that advances have to be paid back if sales do not generate sufficient royalties to 'earn' the advance. This is not true. The publisher's advance is a risk to them, hence the larger the advance, the harder they are likely to try to sell the book.

Normally, a third of the advance is paid on signing the contract, a third on the publication of the hardback (or trade paperback) and the final third on publication of the mass market paperback (mmp). Agents can often plead a case for increasing the percentages at the front end. Needless to say, advances vary enormously and can be as low as £500.   GC

adverb

An adverb is a word that modifies a verb (she laughed *loudly*) or an adjective (she is *very* pretty). An adverb can also modify another adverb, often for emphasis (she walked *very* quickly). Most adverbs are those of manner (*sweetly, straight, perversely*); of degree (*quite, somewhat, really*); or else they are focusing adverbs such as '*only*' or '*even*'.

New writers are often advised to use adverbs sparingly, and to concentrate on their verbs. She *slouched* or *dawdled* is usually judged more telling than she walked *slowly*. Above all, writers are urged to avoid adverbs such as 'very', 'extremely' and 'awfully', sometimes known as 'weak intensifiers'. 'Richard is unusual' is generally thought to be stronger than 'Richard is highly unusual'.

Some writers, like Bernard MacLaverty, excise adverbs almost completely. Others, such as Toni Morrison, believe adverbs distract from dialogue in particular: the skill lies in letting the characters' words convey their tone of voice, rather than writing 'Concita said angrily'. In *Loving*, Henry Green substitutes adjectives for adverbs, writing, for example, 'He went so soft he might have been a ghost without a head' (Green, 2001, p. 9). Adverbs seem at best an optional extra, and at worst the weakest link, detracting from their fellow parts of speech.

But many writers use adverbs with skill and flair. On the cover of his novel *Adverbs*, Daniel Handler (aka Lemony Snicket) declares that 'it is not the nouns. The miracle is the adverbs, the way things are done'. In other words, a well-placed adverb has a unique potential for conveying an action's *how*. At the start of *Bleak House*, for instance, Charles Dickens writes that on a foggy afternoon members of Chancery are '*mistily* engaged in one of the ten thousand stages of an endless cause' (Dickens, 2003, p. 2. Italics mine). Note how his adverb not only reminds us of the fog outside. By delaying and blurring the impact of the verb, it also suggests that his lawyers obscure the facts as the fog obscures the streets.

The closing lines of James Joyce's short story 'The Dead' are both profound and poetic in their description of the central character's painful realization of life's brevity and futility: 'His soul swooned *slowly* as he heard the snow falling *faintly* through the universe and *faintly* falling, like the descent of their last end, upon all the living and the dead' (Joyce, 1996, p. 173. Italics mine). As with the lines from *Bleak House*, a knee-jerk dismissal of adverbs might lead you to underestimate these lines. A swoon, you might say, is unlikely to happen *quickly*, and why does 'faintly' need to be repeated? But Joyce is deploying his adverbs to singular effect. The very superfluity of 'slowly' alerts us to the arrival of 'falling faintly', an alliterative phrase Joyce repeats and inverts in a construction known as chiasmus. Far from diluting its meaning, his adverbs enrich and elevate his verbs, uniting with them to replicate in this desolating conclusion the transformation worked over Ireland by the snow.   *JN*

Further reading
Dickens, Charles, *Bleak House* (London: Penguin, 2003).
Green, Henry, *Loving* (London: Vintage, 2001).
Joyce, James, *Dubliners* (London: Prenguin, 1996).

age

There are no age limits to writing. Mary Shelley completed *Frankenstein* when she was 20 years old in 1818. It was published a year later and remains in print today. The Canadian Alistair MacLeod won the prestigious 2001 IMPAC award for fiction with his first novel, *No Great Mischief*, when he was 65. Many people begin writing as children and continue into old age. Some write for a few years and then stop; others begin late and keep going.

There may be no limits but there are plenty of prejudices about writing and age. For example, that you need experience and maturity before you can write about 'life'. Or that older people shouldn't try to write for a younger audience; and vice versa. Or that young people always write about sex, drugs and rock and roll, while older people write about golf, divorce and death. None of these ideas has validity but, as with gender, race and class, age clearly has an influence on our perspective and experience of the world, and maybe also on the way we use language. However, if you can work a pencil or a word processor and have ideas, skills and commitment, then it doesn't matter when you begin to write or what you write about: you are never too old or too young. *HL*

ageism

Ageism is prejudice or discrimination on the grounds of a person's age. Many people believe that publishers, agents and producers, driven by a youth-obsessed market, favour younger writers regardless of quality or talent. In the United States, in the year 2000, 28 television writers sued the major US TV networks in a class action over claims of age discrimination. They alleged that TV networks often hire only younger writers because of an advertiser-led drive to attract younger audiences. The lawsuit failed but it attracted considerable interest and debate. The literary agent Andrew Lownie, writing on his website about publishing in 2006, says that 'there is a preference for authors who are promotable – young, famous, attractive or preferably all three' (www.andrewlownie.co.uk). Ageism is now probably one of the very few forms of prejudice that is acceptable to express in public, and the writing world is no exception.

Direct discrimination of any kind is damaging and should be resisted. However, ageism can be even more insidious and self-limiting when it is within us: one of those 'mind-forged manacles' that Blake described in his poem 'London'. Writers can make a difference to ageist attitudes by challenging age-based stereotypes in their own writing. That skinhead on the bus may look drug-crazed and violent, but he's actually planning to paddle across the Irish Sea in a bath. And the little old lady in front of him is not kindly and wise – but an 80-year-old who has become a computer hacker to enhance her pension. *HL*

agent

Someone who acts as a filter between the writer and the publisher, selling the work and tending to all the financial and legal details. Agents represent the best interests of your book to the publishing world and will take a 10 to 20 per cent cut of all income (20 per cent for film rights). They will advise you on how best to present the book in terms of quality and commerciality and will strategize how to sell the book to publishers. Generally speaking, the interests of the agent and the writer are inseparable and having an agent is now a necessary, but not necessarily sufficient, condition to getting published.

With publishers being squeezed to operate in an increasingly open and competitive market, much of the creative power within the industry has been devolved to agents. Gone are the days when an aspiring gifted writer could send a script direct to an editor and be discovered. Now, few publishers will countenance direct approaches. To be taken seriously, a script has to be presented by an agent. There are some exceptions and you should refer to the publishers section in the *Writer's Handbook* and/or the *Writers' and Artists' Yearbook*.

As for getting an agent, their details can be found in the *Handbook* and *Yearbook* and a good trick for finding the best agent for you is to select a handful of books which share your own book's genre, tone and audience. Write to the publishers for their catalogues, where you will see which agents represent which books. Call the selected agencies and ask how they like to see work presented (synopses, chapters, whole books by post or email). As a rule, less is more and you should grab an agent's attention, leave them wanting more. Resist the temptation to tell them how many other great ideas you have.

The world of publishing is global, small and incestuous. Your agent will know everybody; and always remember agents need writers as much as we need them. No writers, no deals, and everybody in town is trying to discover the next big thing.   *GC*

alliteration and assonance

Alliteration, the repetition of consonants (usually) at the beginning of words, is the best-known phonemic pattern and part of every schoolchild's poetry kit. It is easy to overuse and can appear childish or obvious. However, some contemporary poets still achieve a powerful effect with their use of this ancient Old English/Old Norse patterning of sound. Assonance, the repetition of vowels, is one of the subtlest forms of phonemic patterning and is used to bring sonic depth to contemporary free verse. Barry MacSweeney's poem 'Pearl's Utter Brilliance' combines alliteration ('whip-winged plovers'), assonance ('heather-crashing feet, splash happy') and compound words ('kneefalls' and 'tumblestones') to create a feeling of joyful energy as he depicts two children in the countryside.   *HT*

Further reading
MacSweeney, Barry, *The Book of Demons* (Newcastle upon Tyne: Bloodaxe Books, 1977).

Amazon

This online bookstore which began in 1994 and only turned a profit ten years later is fast becoming the one-stop shop for many book-buyers. Most of the other big bookstores and publishers have scrambled to keep up, putting their catalogues online and copying Amazon's marketing strategy. Amazon describes itself as 'an online community', and it certainly adds value in a way that conventional bookshops or libraries have up to now been unable to do. There are readers' reviews and favourite lists, as well as tips about books the computer thinks you might be interested in. You can buy and sell second-hand and access practically every book in print without having to move out of your chair. What's not to like?   *HL*
(See **bookshops**)

anachronism

An object, person, activity, etc., which turns up in the wrong time: the clock that chimes in Shakespeare's *Julius Caesar*; a helicopter landing in the eighteenth century. It can also apply to vocabulary or idioms that don't fit the period: a character saying, 'Sorted, man' in 1950. Writers should try to avoid unintended anachronisms, but used deliberately they can be inventive and fun. The TV and comic series *The Flintstones* used wonderful and witty anachronisms all the time: stone-age washing machines and telephones, for example. A helicopter landing in the eighteenth century might be the trigger for a good story.   *HL*

antagonist

(See **protagonist**)

apostrophes

Punctuation mark used to indicate possession or the omission of a letter or number. We are all supposed to learn about them in junior school, but adults who know how to use apostrophes correctly are reasonably rare.

Coffee's is part of what the deli down the road from me advertises on a display board. Such misuse of the apostrophe is precisely what got the goat of Lynne Truss and caused her to write her surprise bestseller about punctuation, *Eats, Shoots & Leaves*. The apostrophe indicates a possessive: *The fountain pen's nib*. And when the owner is plural, the apostrophe follows the 's': *The dogs' home*. Secondly, an apostrophe indicates that a letter (in *can't* and *doesn't*) or numerals in a year (*the winter of '62*) have been omitted.

Perhaps it's possible to understand why people get mixed up about the use of an apostrophe in the two variants of *its*. (*It's* is always short for *it is* or *it has*. *Its* without an apostrophe always indicates possession, that something belongs to 'it'.) However, it's a mystery why anyone would write *coffee's* when what they want to convey is that punters wishing to come inside can buy different kinds of, or more than one, coffee.   RG

Further reading
Truss, Lynne, *Eats, Shoots & Leaves* (London: Profile Books, 2005).

archaisms

Words or constructions no longer in contemporary use. Fiction writers often deliberately use archaisms to convey a particular atmosphere: Mr Ewing, David Mitchell's nineteenth-century character, in his twenty-first-century novel *Cloud Atlas*, writes in his journal, 'I shall describe what befell me this day . . . I slumber not' (Mitchell, 2004, p. 18). There are a couple of archaic words here ('befell', 'slumber') but the formal structure 'I shall' instead of 'I'll' plus the reversed word order ('slumber not') are also convincing, giving the voice historical authenticity. Archaisms are more common in poetry than in any other genre. Some inexperienced writers with fixed ideas about how poetry should sound, often based on nineteenth-century poems studied in childhood, slip into archaisms unknowingly. Some also use archaic constructions or words to make a metre or rhyme scheme work. Lines such as 'Knowst thou the answer to my quest?' are the result. Here we have an inversion of the more common grammatical construction, 'Do you know?', plus the use of an archaic word, 'thou'. Most critics and readers find poetry such as this stilted and off-putting. Ever since the early-twentieth-century modernist revolution in poetry, poets have favoured the language of everyday. The general advice is, avoid.   HL and HT

Further reading
Mitchell, David, *Cloud Atlas* (London: Hodder and Stoughton, 2004).

autobiography

Writing autobiography, sometimes called life writing, can be as inventive a process as writing fiction. Clive James describes his book *Unreliable Memoirs* as 'a disguised novel . . . the whole thing is a figment got up to sound like truth' (James, 1980, p. 9). James is speaking about his own work, but the implication is that all autobiographies can only ever be attempts at the truth. As Ailsa Cox says in 'Writing the Self',

> Autobiography compels through its authenticity. But any literary text is a construct, shaped for its potential readership. Memory itself is selective . . . Memories turn to stories in our heads. Some details are forgotten, while others grow in significance, as we ourselves change and develop. (Cox, in Singleton et al., 1996, p. 78)

When you write about yourself, facts and events have to be ordered and dramatized into a narrative. Other people are necessarily described only from your point of view and choices need to be made about what should be left in or left out. This is not to say that autobiographical writers should feel free to lie or to distort the facts (although, of course, many do!); rather that writing about the self is always partly invented. We may never be able to know ourselves completely: after all, how can 'I' think about 'me' without splitting in two? But writing about your own experience is a way of gaining greater understanding about what it means to be human.

Diaries and journals which explore thoughts and feelings can provide a good basis for autobiographical writing but it is useful to remember that, despite the heightened individualism of our culture, we are not isolated beings, and some of the most interesting autobiographies explore the self in *relationship* to the outer world of people and things. We also need to find a shape for the writing, a focus. For example, in *Toast: The Story of a Boy's Hunger*, Nigel Slater, the cookery author, recounts his childhood and adolescence using different kinds of food. The book is organized in short sections, each with the name of a food as title: *Christmas Cake*; *Sunday Roast*; *Spinach*, etc. This inventive but simple structure successfully intermingles descriptions of good and bad meals, family occasions and the author's often difficult relationship with his parents. Francis Spufford's book *The Child that Books Built* traces his growing up through his love of reading, through all the story worlds he inhabited as a boy.

Nigel Slater and Francis Spufford are drawing on a familiar organizing technique that many of us practised in the composition exercises we had to do at school: 'All the foods I love and hate'; 'Best holidays'; 'Favourite books'; 'Pets I have known', etc. Such activities may seem naive but they offer a useful model to the adult autobiographical writer. Think of your own strong likes and dislikes, obsessions and habits, as breadcrumbs leading you, like Hansel and Gretel, into the forest of memories. As you follow them, writing them down, sooner or later you'll make out a faint track: a narrative path though your life.   *HL*

(See **blogs**)

Writing ideas

Write about your childhood through things or specific experiences, e.g. shoes you loved – or hated; sweets; houses you lived in; favourite toys or games; music; friends; dens; pets.

- First, list as many of the particular objects, places, people, etc.
- Jot down a few notes about each. Try to think back to how you experienced them, *as a child.* This may be difficult – as we become adults, we often begin to romanticize or demonize childhood. Try to step back into the child's world.
- Now write an autobiographical piece, using these objects or experiences as stepping stones towards a narrative which explores the particular child you were. The aim is to retain the freshness and honesty of the child's vision with the insight, distance and complexity of the adult perspective.
- A warning. Revisiting childhood can be painful and difficult for some people. If the material is too raw and private, or you are not ready to explore it, feel free to write only about the areas that are less challenging.

Further reading

Cox, Ailsa, 'Writing the Self', in Singleton, J., et al., *The Creative Writing Handbook* (London: Macmillan, 1996).

James, Clive, *Unreliable Memoirs* (London: Picador, 1980).

Slater, Nigel, *Toast* (London: Harper Perennial, 2004).

Spufford, Francis, *The Child That Books Built* (London: Faber, 2000).

automatic writing

This is a technique which attempts to bypass the rational mind. The Surrealists did a lot of it, probably under the influence of drink or drugs, although spiritualists who hoped the dead might send them a message also favoured it. Here's what you do.

Take a pen or pencil – it won't work with a word processor – and a blank piece of paper. Begin writing while trying not to think. It might work for you but it usually produces only illegible gobbledegook for me. Trying to switch off consciousness while awake and sober is probably impossible. However, a more productive version is to write for a timed period without planning or censoring. Try it. You don't need to believe in the id or the ether. Sometimes writing just writes itself.   *HL*

ballad

An important **poetic genre**, the ballad has been with us since the fifteenth century, both as a popular verse form in its own right and as an inspiration to writers such as Wordsworth and Coleridge. Ballads were originally songs or stories with a strong narrative thread, often relating the story of a local disaster or legend. They have always been memorized and performed in public, hence the form, a memorable pattern of interlacing four- and three-stress lines with a strong rhyme scheme and repeated lines and phrases.

The ballad gave birth to modern folk music and, since the 1960s, has had a strong influence on pop music too. Bob Dylan, Joni Mitchell, Janis Ian and many other '60s singer-songwriters drew inspiration from it. Dylan's song 'A Hard Rain's A-Gonna Fall' is very closely related in form and language to the Scottish ballad 'Lord Randal'. Dylan's 'Oh, where have you been, my blue-eyed son?' derives directly from 'Oh where ha' you been, Lord Randal my son?' and the song continues with a series of related questions and answers and a repeated chorus at the end of each stanza. In this way, the ballad writer (ancient or modern) builds up momentum, rhythm and suspense. It's also worth checking out Nick Cave's album *Murder Ballads*, inspired by the sub-genre of ballads concerned with gruesome crime stories. If you write narrative poems or pop lyrics, it's well worth looking into the ballad.   *HT*

Further reading

Friedmann, A. B., *The Penguin Book of Folk Ballads of the English-Speaking World* (London: Penguin, 1982).

Wordsworth, William and Samuel Taylor Coleridge, *Lyrical Ballads* (1798), eds R. L. Brett and A. R. Jones (London: Routledge, 1991).

beginning

The first word is always diffic . . . You sit down at a desk and you . . . Many writers, including me, have problems with . . .

beginning

We open a finished piece of work and look at those neat printed sentences and we half-consciously imagine that is how they have been from the start: words arriving perfectly formed out of the mouth of God, or Nature, through the medium of that magical creature, the Author. Listen to Mary Shelley describing how she came by the idea for her novel *Frankenstein*:

> The witching hour had gone by, before we retired to rest . . . My imagination, unbidden, possessed and guided me. . . . I saw the hideous phantasm of a man stretched out, and then, on the working of some powerful engine, show signs of life, and stir with an uneasy, half vital motion. (Shelley, 1994: Preface, p. 7)

Note that phrase: *'My imagination unbidden, possessed and guided me.'* The **Romantic** ideology, with its emphasis on heart over head, rather than formal discipline, often segues into the appealing but mistaken idea that the imagination is *all* that is needed to begin writing. Being guided, unbidden, by a mysterious entity seems a much easier way to produce a novel than having to actually write the thing. What Mary Shelley didn't go on to describe was that nerve-wracking moment the next day when she sat down at a table and after sharpening her quill and looking out of the window and sharpening her quill *again* and looking out of the window *again*, she had to make that first mark: to begin. *I was born in . . . My father was . . . I am by birth a Genovese.*

For many writers that first mark isn't the real beginning at all. There needs to be a spark, something that triggers an idea: a snatch of speech overheard; a gesture; a nagging memory. Henry James refers to this trigger as a germ, a seed:

> Most of the stories straining to shape under my hands have sprung from a single small seed, a seed as minute and wind-blown as that casual hint for *The Spoils of Poynton* dropped unwittingly by my neighbour, a mere floating particle in the stream of talk. (James, in Allott, 1965, p. 138)

Any conversation, any moment, offers the possibility of an idea, a beginning, but you do have to be listening, to be ready to receive it; and such readiness needs not only attention but also a relaxed and open mind. There are many ways to get in touch with this state of fertile relaxation: music or silence; a room of your own or a noisy bar; a certain necessary detachment from the stream of talk perhaps. Some people lie in the bath. Tolstoy, author of *War and Peace*, believed that morning walks helped.

> I always write in the morning. I was pleased to hear lately that Rousseau too, after he got up in the morning, went for a short walk and sat down to work . . . The best thoughts most often come in the morning after waking, while still in bed or during the walk. (Tolstoy, in Allott, 1965, p. 150)

Once you've got the idea, then you have to write it down. Another beginning. The white page can be as enticing as fresh snow or as bleak as the Arctic and there is nothing quite like a blank screen with its impatient, foot-tapping cursor, to make the mind go blank too. But remember that the first marks are not the beginnings of your story, but the beginnings of the first **draft** of your story. It is comforting to realize that words can be rewritten and that horribly malformed sentences can disappear with a mouse click. You can always begin again.

Every story, poem, novel, script – every good piece of writing – has at least three beginnings: the first is the germ, the idea that kick-starts something into growth; the second is the first draft: words staggering out of bed, unbrushed, unshowered, not yet fit for man, woman or beast to look at; the third beginning is the one that belongs to the reader, the one you see when you open the book: neat, sweet and squeaky clean on the page; every word combed; every sentence flossed. Writing is what happens in between.   *HL*

Writing ideas

1. Use the alphabet to write down a list of words: *ant*; *blue*; *custard*; *danger*; *elephant*; *fish*; *Google*. When you reach *z*, read them over and pick three that appeal to you. Choose two **concrete** words and one **abstract** word. Now write a paragraph using all three words. Try this a few times, using the same words in each one until you've got a few paragraphs. All these paragraphs are possible beginnings.
2. Experiment with **point of view**, sometimes beginning with the **first person**: *I watched the ant pick its way carefully over the skin of the custard*; sometimes with the **third person**: *He hated school. The ugly navy-blue uniform; lumpy custard; the dangerous playground.* Read them through and see if they resonate. Maybe some of the paragraphs can be linked together. Now write the next paragraph. Then the next.

Further reading

Allott, Miriam, *Novelists on the Novel* (London: Routledge, 1965).

Shelley, Mary, *Frankenstein* (1831) (London: Penguin, 1994).

being a writer

Many of us use this expression when we begin to write, sometimes even before we have done any serious writing. 'I want to be a writer', we say. 'Being a writer is what I've always dreamed of.' It's worth pausing for a moment to think about what we mean by this.

Although it is commonly used to refer to professions and activities, the verb *to be* also has a static and passive quality: after all, you can just *be* a woman, a Glaswegian, a 20-year-old without having to make any effort at all. A lot of people imagine, often unconsciously, that *being a writer* is a bit like being a member of an inclusive and secretive society: all you need is a funny handshake, a golden key and you're in. Behind that secret door, you will find the way to freely express yourself, ideas will blossom, and words will flow, along with the cash and celebrity.

It's not surprising that many of us have these notions. The idea that the artist (composer; painter; poet) is an exceptional *being* set apart from the rest of us, with their own artistic aura, is a powerful theme within society. Of course, a moment's rational consideration should expose this as largely ridiculous but we are not always rational: the dream of being a member of that exclusive society persists in the cultural unconscious.

Wanting to *be* a writer can be helpful: it can drive ambition and increase effort. On the other hand, it can be a hindrance; undermining confidence and giving people a false picture of what is needed. Better to focus on the more active verbs: *do*; *write*. After all, you can develop and improve the way you *do* things. You may not feel much like a creative genius; you may not even feel like a writer, but you can just keep writing. This is what writers *do*: they sit down in front of the page, the screen, curious, afraid. Words appear one after another. They cross them out, they look at what they've written, they write more. Not being, but doing. HL

bestsellers

The fastest selling books in a given period and the trade's most accepted barometer of success. Bestseller lists can be found in the review sections of the weekend press, in *The Bookseller* magazine, and are summarized annually in the *Writers' and Artists' Yearbook*.

As in most walks of life, success breeds success and having 'bestseller' on the jacket of your book will probably be a self-fulfilling strapline. Bestsellers make life easy for everybody in the chain, from your agent when he or she is selling the book, to editors when they are getting the authority to bid for it, and the booksellers when they are negotiating with the bookshops to take two hundred copies rather than two! (Remember, it is the size of the pile and the proximity to the door or till which determines a book's commercial success far more than reviews and artistry.)

Bestsellers can be anything from *Harry Potter* and *The Da Vinci Code* to *The Little Book of God Knows What* or Jordan's autobiography. The lists will often exclude such stealth sellers as the Bible and *The Highway Code*.   GC

blank page

Fear of the blank screen or page is common among writers. It has to do with the adventure into the unknown, with the pressure of creating something new in the world more or less from scratch. The one cure I know for this is getting into a routine of sitting down to write on a regular basis. Once your unconscious becomes attuned to your producing 1,000 words – or whatever it is – a day, fear of the blank screen will be greatly diminished. A regular routine will mean that you aren't faced with producing anything from scratch – at least, not after the first day.   RG

(See **block**)

block

Depending on your point of view, *writer's block* can be a painful psychological disturbance or a self-deluding excuse. The term has acquired a semi-medical status, similar to tennis elbow or housemaid's knee: sounding like a disease or affliction that can be diagnosed, treated and cured. This medicalized model was developed within psychoanalytical circles in the first half of the twentieth century: psychoanalysts, from Freud onwards, treated writers who could not write by searching out complexes within the unconscious mind. Soon, as with many other psychological terms and syndromes, the notion of a specific and clearly definable syndrome unique to writers became firmly rooted in popular culture. And despite the unpleasant connotations, it was, and still is, a surprisingly popular complaint: unlike haemorrhoids or varicose veins (all that sitting!), writer's block is a stylish explanation for failing to meet a deadline: the writer's equivalent of a sick note.

block

The idea of writer's block as a full-blown neurosis is probably no longer meaningful to most of us, but most writers suffer from self-doubt and loss of confidence at times. The word 'block' has powerful and ominous connotations of heaviness and stasis: 'an obstruction which makes movement or flow difficult or impossible', says the dictionary. It helps to know that many writers have had the same experiences and have overcome them. Virginia Woolf records in her diary the struggle to get started:

How am I to begin it? And what is it to be? I feel no great impulse, no fever; only a great pressure of difficulty. Why write it then? Why write at all? (Woolf, 1953, in Allot, 1965, p. 142)

And even when you've finally begun to write, the flow can dry up in the middle. Joseph Conrad, author of *Heart of Darkness*, speaks of how

in the course of [a] working day of eight hours I write three sentences which I erase before leaving the table in despair . . . it takes all my resolution and power of self-control to refrain from butting my head against the wall. (Conrad, 1988, 2: 49)

Zachary Leader, in *Writer's Block*, notes that blockage takes many forms but these are forms with common features, which he loosely defines as internal and external. Internal blockages are experienced as individual, psychological weaknesses: a lack of faith in your own ability; uncertainty about your 'right' to be a writer; judging yourself too harshly; being unable to begin at all or to bring a piece to a resolution, etc.

External blockages have a number of origins: some related to the literary world itself, to *The Anxiety of Influence*, as Harold Bloom described it. We are introduced as children to the 'greats' of literature: Shakespeare; Charles Dickens; J. D. Salinger. How could we possibly compete with such literary heroes? And as we sit down to write, we can't help but be aware of all those other writers, the books being churned out in their millions every day, the bookshop shelves groaning under the weight of new titles. What could we add? What could we possibly say that hasn't already been said?

Then there is the **Romantic** idea that writers need to be 'inspired', to be touched by dreams or the imaginative muse before they can get started; after all, Wordsworth seems to have spotted that host of dancing daffodils while wandering around the Lake District, 'lonely as a cloud'. Easy-peasy.

Don't you believe it. An idea is one thing; writing is another. Wordsworth's daffodils were actually seen by his sister, Mary, and he, of course, wrote his poems at his desk like the rest of us, probably with plenty of crossings-out.

External factors such as class, race and gender can also be major blocks. Tillie Olson's *Silences* records in detail the effects of isolation and self-doubt on many 'non-traditional' writers: 'Literary history and the present are dark with silences . . . some silences hidden . . . some never coming to book form at all' (Olson, 1980, p. 6). This is partly economic. As Olson comments, 'Substantive creative work takes time, and with rare exceptions only full-time workers have achieved it' (Olson, 1980, p. 17).

You have to have enough money to buy time to write but in order to get money, you need a job, which takes up all your writing time. This is why there are fewer writers living on council estates than in wealthy London suburbs or on university campuses. It's not only about money though: if you believe that writing 'belongs' to certain fixed groups – white people, geniuses, French absinthe drinkers – then you're likely to experience blockages if you're not one of them. Here the internal and external factors merge into each other: the things we tell ourselves, true or false, have a habit of becoming self-fulfilling.

But what is to be done? The name – *writer's block* – lends a mysterious power to painful but practical difficulties without giving much guidance about how to deal with them. There are many useful tactics for overcoming these difficulties, some of which you will find elsewhere in this book and in the further recommended reading. The best advice is to stop thinking and just do it. Badly if necessary.   HL

Writing ideas
1. Resolve to write for a certain period of time: half an hour; an hour; two hours, etc. If you find you can't manage that, then *shorten* the period of time: fifteen minutes; ten minutes; two minutes, etc. Write by the clock and stop when the time is up. It doesn't matter whether you write anything significant or good. Do this until you feel frustrated with having to stop. Sex therapists use a similar technique for couples who have lost their libido. The idea is to make you hot for writing.
2. Pay attention to the way you think and establish your own set of ideas and values. Unlearn all those stories about writers being part of a privileged group and inwardly assert your own entitlement to write.

Further reading

Conrad, Joseph, *Collected Letters*, ed. Frederick R. Karl (Cambridge: Cambridge University Press, 1988).

Leader, Zachary, *Writer's Block* (London: John Hopkins, 1991).

Olson, Tillie, *Silences* (London: Virago, 1980).

blog

A blog, derived from web-log, is an online journal or diary, with regular entries presented in reverse date order. You can also use 'blog' as a verb: *to blog* means to write up your blog. According to the listing site *Technorati*, there were over 17 million blogs in September 2006, covering a huge range of subjects. Many follow personal journeys mainly of interest for family, friends and colleagues, while others focus on subjects that gain a wider following. News and journalistic agencies are increasingly incorporating blog material into mainstream and online reporting and in 2005, many blogs provided first-hand accounts of Hurricane Katrina as it hit New Orleans.

Anyone can create a blog for themselves by using a dedicated blog-hosting service such as e-blogger. Most blogs are text-based although many also contain images and sound, plus links to other blogs or websites. The relevance for writers is that blogs offer a space to try out your work, to meet other writers and to explore ideas about writing. Even if you don't want to write a blog yourself, there are helpful resources and an online community of people interested in writing. Blogs offer an unmediated way to reach an audience, but the same rules apply as in normal publication: you have to have something interesting to write about and you have to write it well. *HL*

Useful websites

e-blogger: www.blogger.com

Technorati: www.technorati.com/blogs

bookshops

A well-stocked bookshop is useful for carrying out research on publication, particularly when planning to write non-fiction. Search for books that are similar to yours and note the names of their publishers. The big chains like Waterstone's and Barnes and Noble are great places for readers but a little bit scary for many writers. Floor-to-ceiling heaps of new fiction can be daunting when you're stuck in the middle of your first novel without a publisher in sight. Small independent bookshops are rarer but also have added value for

writers: some will promote local authors and publications, as well as advertising groups and events. Many people buy books online these days but there's nothing to beat the serendipity of bookshop browsing to actually hold those objects in your hand and smell the ink. Use 'em or lose 'em.   *HL*
(See **Amazon**)

breathing space

The use of **section-breaks** and, for that matter, **chapters**, offers the reader some breathing space, and in that space she can rest from reading, and perhaps allow her unconscious to process the information that has gone before the break. It's preferable to cut your fiction up into sections which have some relation to the attention span of the human mind. Using dual or **multiple viewpoint** has a similar effect; the reader is having a breather from character A when you move to the viewpoint of character B.   *RG*

caricature

In literature or illustration this refers to a person whose distinguishing characteristics are exaggerated to create a ridiculous or bizarre effect. The ugly sisters in *Cinderella* are so ugly they become funny; the English, in some American films, either speak in upper-class accents and drink tea or speak in cockney accents and drink tea; most of the characters in the TV series *Little Britain* are caricatures. Caricature can be a useful dramatic technique but needs to be used carefully. Miss Havisham in Dickens' *Great Expectations* is an exaggerated version of the spurned half-mad woman, but she retains her gothic menace, never quite slipping over the line into bathos.   *HL*
(See **stereotype**)

change

A fundamental ingredient of narrative is change. This may be to do with action and situation: somebody does something and as a result the world in the story is altered. It may also be to do with perception. The protagonist's view of another character, or of himself, is changed in the course of the story. The villain's heroic side is glimpsed, or vice versa. Similarly, readers' understanding of the protagonist or the situation may change as they read on.

You've heard of the plot thickening; this is as a result of things changing. The alternative is things staying the same, which readers won't like. How do you introduce change in your narratives? You may find it helpful to think in terms of plot development. The situation at any moment in a story may be as dramatic as you like but it can't stay the same; it must develop. You might approach this by asking *What if . . . ?* questions. The heroine and her husband can't have children; what if she finds an abandoned baby? Bear in mind as you ask these questions that change in your plot ought to introduce a gradual increase in the conflict.   *RG*

chaos

Edward Lorenz's work on computerized weather prediction in 1961 led to him theorizing that the flap of a butterfly's wing could sufficiently change atmospheric conditions to set in motion a tornado on the far side of the world. The butterfly effect, or chaos theory, is pertinent to writers: one seemingly insignificant shift in the initial balance of a narrative can add up to immense changes in the end. Chaos is also the creative state when there is much material and no apparent order, but this is often the necessary mess out of which progress emerges: look for the happy accident; never underestimate the value of play. *HN*

chapters

Subdivisions in books. The end of a chapter signals to the reader that a pause is possible here. Chapters are similar to movements in symphonies, each one containing a complete phase within the greater narrative of the book. The shift from one chapter to the next may also be a way of facilitating the move from one time-period or one location to another. However, not all novels are divided into chapters. You can, in the manner of Daniel Defoe, write in an uninterrupted stream of **narrative**. Also possible is making a division larger than the chapter: breaking a novel into three or four 'parts', each of which includes chapters, and suggesting that each part represents something relatively complete within itself. A novel in three parts suggests a nod towards the three-act play, or, more simply, towards a **beginning**, **middle** and end (see **endings**) structure.

The conventional way to label chapters is numerically: *Chapter 1.* (Or just: *1.*) That this is a literary endeavour may be communicated by putting it so: *Chapter One.* Or, more economically, thus: *One.* Some authors like to name a chapter, too, as Amy Tan does here: *8: Too Much Yin.* Most modish of all is to indicate a new chapter by nothing more than taking a fresh page and beginning one third of the way down. *RG*

(See also **white space**)

characters

Story people. Characters are the single most important element in fiction. Every aspect of fiction writing – plot, dialogue, voice – is significant, but characters are paramount. What are they, what are characters in fiction? One thing they are not is people. At one level, a character is ink on a page. Less reductively, a character is a great deal simpler than you or me. Characters in fiction have a limited range of attributes. As Helen Newall has pointed out, characters in fiction are *edited.* (Why? Because if they were as complicated and sophisticated as real human beings they would not be sufficiently comprehensible to function in a work of fiction.) Not only are characters edited, but they are also dramatized. James N. Frey (1988) puts the case for characters being bigger, better, stronger, more courageous, more extreme than real people.

Characters mainly come from life. Readers like characters to be recognizable from their own experience. However, characters in fiction are not always based on a single person and may be conflations of real people; authors frequently build characters out of details taken from a number of people they know. (And you don't even need to know them; it's perfectly possible to lift a characteristic, or a whole character, from someone only glimpsed in a café.)

Once you have a character in mind, how do you convey who they are to your readers? Three simple and effective ways – perhaps the best ways to do it – are to focus on what your characters say, what they do and how they appear.

In Marina Lewycka's novel *A Short History of Tractors in Ukrainian*, we learn a good deal about Valentina, the gold-digger who is after the narrator's elderly father, from her appearance:

> Then I see her – a large blonde woman, sauntering down the garden towards us on high-heeled, peep-toed mules. Her gait is lazy, contemptuous, as though she can barely be bothered to stir herself to greet us. A denim mini-skirt rides high above her knees; a pink sleeveless top stretches around voluptuous breasts that bob up and down as she walks. (Lewycka, 2005, p. 76)

We also come to know her through what she says, and the way she says it: 'Why you want for talk?', for example, or: 'Your father buy me nothing! No car! No jewel! No clothes! No cosmetic!' But perhaps most of all we get to know Valentina through what she does (spending the old man's limited funds on three useless cars, running a couple of other men on the side) and the way she behaves (mostly with considerable aggression).

Characters are also created through association with their surroundings. The setting of the fiction, for instance, may say a great deal about who they are. The tacky Los Angeles setting of Zoë Heller's 1999 novel *Everything You Know* says a good deal about the washed-up English writer Willy Muller who finds himself marooned there late in life. This characterization by association may also be seen in Solzhenitsyn's *One Day In The Life of Ivan Denisovich* (1963), where the Soviet prison camp says much about who the protagonist is – suffering, abused, impersonalized. Similarly, the props associated with a character may signify things to the reader, which relates to the term Scholes and Kellog coined when writing of Henry James: 'solidity of specification' (1966). Specification creates solidity, as in this extract from Carol Shields' *Larry's Party*, which focuses on Larry's trade, floristry:

> Flowerfolks is a small chain with a reputation for friendly service and a quality product. Usually you can spot a Flowerfolks arrangement by its natural appearance. For instance, they don't go in for bending stems into far-out shapes and positions, or for those Holly Hobby wreathes et cetera, or weird combinations like, say, tulips and birds-of-paradise sticking out of the same arrangement. Even their Welcome-New-Baby floral offerings have a fresh earthy look to them. Larry says it makes him shudder just thinking about those Styrofoam lamb shapes with pink and blue flowers . poking out of their backs. (Shields, 1998, p. 61)

The specific details about Larry's workplace inform our understanding of his character – especially when, as in that last sentence, his intelligent, contemporary thoughts intersect with those details.

One character is often created through another, which enables a double characterization: what a viewpoint character notices about other characters helps us to understand those observed, but also reveals something about the viewpoint character. In this passage from *For Kings and Planets* by Ethan Canin, the different worlds of Orno Tarcher, the viewpoint character, and Marshall Emerson, his new friend, are opened up in this short snatch of dialogue.

> 'I'm glad to see you wake up at this hour, too,' he said. 'Where I'm from, everybody does, but around here nobody seems to.'
> Marshall stared back at him. 'Oh, you're really not kidding, are you?'
> Orno looked back, smiling unsteadily.
> 'I'm not waking up,' said Marshall. 'I'm getting home.' (Canin, 1999, p. 5)

The focus is on Marshall, whom Orno has just met, but at least as much is revealed about Orno – he is being naive, he keeps more conventional hours.

At the outset, I put forward the view that character is the most important aspect of fiction writing. One reason for this is that it is from your characters and their situations that your plot will come. Understanding character is the secret of plotting. If you know your protagonist inside out, then you will know how he or she will respond in any given situation. Henry James put it more elegantly: 'What is character but the determination of incident? What is incident but the illustration of character?' (James, ed. Shapiro, 1963, p. 131). A narrative where the characters have been squeezed into a carefully constructed plot may not be credible or satisfying for the reader, but one that is character-led has the authenticity of the inevitable. In short, it's impossible to know your characters too well, and fully understanding them will often be the secret of successful plotting.   *RG*

(See also **revision**)

Writing ideas

1. *Minor characters*

   Every piece of fiction has its walk-on parts. Here are a few ways of developing some. A character with an odd hobby – collecting beer-mats or perfume bottles. All that need distinguish a minor character is a physical characteristic. Think of the skin. The novel I'm reading compares the texture of an old man's skin to greaseproof paper. An item of clothing may be all you need to bring a walk-on character alive. How about somebody who wears driving gloves? Using these examples as your stimulus, come up with three minor characters and store them away in your journal for future use.

2. *Way of speaking*

   Valentina, the vamp in *A Short History of Tractors in Ukrainian*, is in part characterized by the way she speaks. Think of somebody you know who has a particularly striking way of speaking. Now start to develop a character from this, using some dialogue. If necessary, exaggerate the idiosyncrasies of this character's way of speaking.

3. *Building blocks*

   This character drives an E-Class Mercedes, plays polo, holidays in the Dordogne and likes to go to the opera. You have a pretty clear view of who he is already, haven't you? Here are a handful of blocks with which you can build a character of your own: kind of house she lives in; TV programme she won't miss; kind of school her daughter attends; supermarket she shops in; how (and if) she exercises; newspaper she reads; artist she has most CDs by. Of course, you can design your own building blocks for developing characters indefinitely.

Further reading

Canin, Ethan, *For Kings and Planets* (London: Bloomsbury, 1999).

Frey, James N., *How To Write A Damn Good Novel* (London: MacMillan, 1988).

Heller, Zoë, *Everything You Know* (London: Viking, 1999).

James, Henry, 'The Art of Fiction', collected in Morris Shapira (ed.), *Henry James: Selected Literary Criticism* (Harmondsworth: Penguin, 1963).

Lewycka, Marina, *A Short History of Tractors in Ukrainian* (London: Doubleday, 2005).

Scholes, Robert and Robert Kellog, *The Nature of Narrative* (Oxford: Oxford University Press, 1966).

Shields, Carol, *Larry's Party* (London: Fourth Estate, 1998).

Solzhenitsyn, Alexander, *One Day In The Life of Ivan Denisovich* (Harmondsworth: Penguin, 1963).

children, writing for

There are a number of essential elements needed when writing for children. The first is to keep the story moving. As Philip Pullman, author of the best-selling *His Dark Materials* trilogy, puts it on his website, 'Writing for a younger readership forces you not to let the story go out of your mind. If you stop telling a story, they stop reading.' The second is not to talk down to or patronize your readers. The third is to be aware of the age range you are writing for: there's a huge difference between picture books for under-fives, adventure stories for ten-year-olds and books that explore relationships for adolescents. However, there is no need to be rigid about age: many seven-year-olds love stories aimed at threes to nines and there are also plenty of adults reading *Alice in Wonderland* and *Harry Potter.*

We were all children once. This obvious truth is the best starting point when writing for children, but for many of us it is also the biggest barrier. Adults often idealize or demonize their own youth, remembering only the happy or the tragic times, forgetting that what really appeals to the child is not the moral or the psychological meaning of the story but the story itself. The children's writer needs to re-inhabit the pragmatic and fantastic imagination of a seven- or eleven-year-old, while at the same time keeping a mature control of the planning, writing and editing process. This is as difficult as patting your head and rubbing your tummy.

There are lots of books and websites which give advice on how to write for children, many of them useful. However, before you write a word, the best thing you can do is to go into the children's library, choose an armful of the most popular books and begin to read. Become that child again. You know you want to. *HL*

Further reading
Philip Pullman at www.philip-pullman.com/about_the_writing.asp.

class

Like race, gender, sexuality, etc., class is another way of categorizing people according to social and economic position. It used to be a bad thing for a writer to be working class and now it's often a bad thing to be middle class, which is surprising as most of us are. In the 1960s and '70s, groups were set up to develop 'working-class' writing, mainly local history, poetry and autobiography. The Federation of Worker Writers and Community Publishers (FWWCP) began in 1976 and is still going strong. See their website at www.thefwwcp.org.uk. Interestingly the organization has dropped the not very fashionable word, class, from its promotional material, preferring the vaguer and safer terms *people* and *community*. Whatever the nomenclature, the key is wider opportunity for people who might otherwise not have access to writers' groups. Some of the federated groups run competitions and give publishing opportunities to local writers. As Tom Paine said, 'The Republic of Letters is more ancient than monarchy'; or, you don't have to be posh and rich to write.   *HL*

Further reading
Federation of Worker Writers and Community Publishers: www.thefwwcp.org.uk.

cliché

To take the bull by the horns and leave no stone unturned, a cliché is an expression that is overused and lacking in originality: the turkey twizzler of writing: cheap and easy junk food with little nourishment. *Oil the wheels*; *grind to a halt*; *add insult to injury*; *warts and all*; *sick as a parrot*. David Crystal describes clichés as zombies: 'fragments of language apparently dying, yet unable to die' (Crystal, 2003, p. 186).

The general view is that a person who talks or writes in clichés is either not very good at language, like a stereotypical footballer, or trying to avoid giving a straight answer, like a shifty politician.

Many clichés have become such a part of everyday expression that it takes an effort to notice they are images at all: *to break the ice*, *to go out of your way*, etc. Language is cluttered with these broken-off bits of old images that help us connect with each other without too much effort or thought. Clichés have been useful since time immemorial: many conversations would grind to a halt without them: they help to oil the social wheels. After all is said and done, we can't all be original all the time and your fictional characters will certainly need clichés if they are to tell it like it is. The trick is to spot when you're using them, to cut out the ones that don't work, to keep the ones that do, and be able to distinguish one from t'other. At the end of the day.   *HL*

Further reading

Crystal, David, *The Cambridge Encyclopedia of the English Language* (Cambridge: Cambridge University Press, 2003).

climax

The point of greatest intensity in a story, film or play. The word originates in the Latin for *ladder* which gives an indication of the way a narrative may develop through a series of lesser climaxes building up to the big one. In a conventional plot structure the main climax comes about two-thirds through, when the protagonist is in such trouble they look unlikely to survive/escape/find out the truth, etc. The climax is the point at which all is at stake. It won't have escaped anyone's notice that the term also refers to orgasm and some writers actually manage to neatly combine these two meanings together by making the – er – climax happen when the estranged lovers finally get together.   *HL*

clutter

Superfluous words. Most of what needs to be said about clutter was put in a letter of 1899 by Anton Chekhov:

> You understand it at once when I say, 'The man sat on the grass'; you understand it because it is clear and makes no demands on the attention.
> On the other hand, it is not easily understood, and it is difficult for the mind, if I write, 'A tall, narrow-chested, middle-sized man, with a red beard, sat on the green grass, already trampled by pedestrians, sat silently, shyly, and timidly looked about him.'
> That is not immediately grasped by the mind, whereas good writing should be grasped at once – in a second. (Letter to Maxim Gorky, 3 September 1899)

In other words, less is more. Clutter is avoided by cutting down on the extraneous, so you might take some of Strunk and White's advice from *The* concrete

Elements of Style (1999) (see also **style**) by writing with verbs and nouns (because adjectives and adverbs can clutter) and avoiding qualifying phrases – get it right first time. William Zinsser, author of *On Writing Well*, defines clutter as 'the laborious phrase which has pushed out the short word that means the same thing'. Prioritizing economy and simplicity in your writing are ways of keeping clutter at bay. Removing clutter is one of the principal tasks when redrafting.   RG

(See **description**)

Further reading

Chekhov, Anton, letter to Maxim Gorky, 3 September 1899, from *Anton Chekhov on Writing*, Nebraska Centre for Writers, www.mockingbird.creighton.edu/NCW/chekwrit.htm (accessed 25 April 2006).
Zinsser, William, *On Writing Well* (New York: HarperCollins, 2006).

concrete

Most of us would recognize this stuff if a block of it hit us on the head, but the word's broader meaning refers to anything which is physical or material. In relation to language, a concrete word is one that describes something that can be experienced through the senses. Examples: nose-ring; coffee; smoke; lemon. There are degrees of concrete-ness. *Colour*, for instance, is abstract: as you don't know which colour it is, you can't see it, even in imagination. *Red* is concrete. But to a person with a strong visual sense, *crimson*, *ox-blood*, and *scarlet* invoke even more powerful sense-impressions of redness. Concrete-rich language makes it easier for the reader to slide between the words and live in the story. Not an animal but a dog. Not a dog, but a black whippet. Not a sound; but a yelping bark. Not a doggy smell but the stink of wet fur and meaty teeth.   HL

conflict

Tension that generates narrative. The engine of **drama** and **narrative**, conflict 'often occurs when two characters have mutually exclusive aims' (Dave Jackson in Newman et al., 2004, p. 70): Van Helsing and Count Dracula in *Dracula*, for instance. Another way of looking at it is to say that conflict is about two strong forces meeting; the reason that this creates drama has to do with the fact that we wonder who will come out on top. Conflict need not necessarily evolve from two characters; it often arises between character and situation: James Stewart's character, who is afraid of heights, is forced to go to the top of a tower at the climax of the film *Vertigo*. However, perhaps the most common source of conflict is that which arises in the **simple linear plot** – from characters struggling to overcome the obstacles which impede their progress towards their goal. In *Cold Mountain*, the conflict arises from Inman's struggle to triumph over everything that prevents him getting home to Ada.

As you feel the pulse in the conflict of your narrative, ask yourself 'What's at stake?' If you want to engage and retain your reader, something has to matter, to sustain a question in the minds of readers. If your protagonist is a bank robber, besieged in a bank by the police, it's clear that plenty is at stake, but if he's a schoolteacher who wants to finish a pile of marking in time to watch *Coronation Street*, perhaps not enough is at stake. And there's a point worth emphasizing: your conflict situation will often have to have a degree of drama greater than most of us encounter in the daily round. Ian McEwan's *Enduring Love* opens with a man trying to prevent a hot-air balloon with a boy in its basket from escaping. He is clinging to a rope attached to the rising balloon. Not something that happens to many people; but often, if it is to be dramatic, fiction will be like that.

James N. Frey speaks of three kinds of conflict, only one of which is desirable:

> conflict which fails to rise is *static* — any kind of conflict which is unchanging. Conflict which rises too quickly is *jumping* — it leaps from one level of intensity to another without adequate motivation or transitional stages. What the dramatist wants is slowly rising conflict which reveals more facets of character because the characters will react differently at each stage of the conflict. As the character responds to rising conflict, he changes, showing all of his colours. Conflict proves character. (Frey, 1988, pp. 40–2)

Sometimes, conflict may be internal: your protagonist is placed in a dilemma by harbouring two desires that are mutually opposed: part of Hamlet wants to avenge his father, but another part does not.   *RG*

Writing idea
Think of that situation in *Vertigo*: a man with a fear of heights who is forced to climb to the top of a tall building. Now come up with a character who has a debilitating fear and put him in a situation that is the worst possible for a

person with this particular fear. Write a couple of pages of conflict-packed fiction.

Further reading

Newman, Jenny, Edmund Cusick and Aileen La Tourette (eds), *The Writer's Workbook* (London: Arnold, 2004).
McEwan, Ian, *Enduring Love* (London: Vintage, 1997).
Frey, James N., *How To Write A Damn Good Novel* (London: Macmillan, 1988).

craft

The skills you acquire which allow you to make a written work of art which has particular effects on the reader. Craft is knowing what you have to do in order to affect readers the way you want to affect them. (You might be said to be crafty if you could pull that one off.)

If you are a student in the subject area of Creative Writing, craft is both an aspect and an outcome of your curriculum. You study the craft deployed by contemporary practitioners as well as some of the theories writers and teachers have evolved about how to write, and you practise writing in order that you may, in turn, develop your own craft.   RG

creative process

The journey a writer and a piece of writing take from idea to final draft. Creativity is a process in which ideas evolve over time and with work. It is a process which currently exercises the minds of researchers and their MRI scanners. Thus far, there seems to be consensus that it involves distinct stages distinguishable in the labs by differing patterns of brain activity. In his 1959 work, *Creativity and Its Cultivation*, Erich Fromm noted that creativity requires firstly the ability to be puzzled, whereas George Kneller proposed that the first stage was finding and/or formulating the problem. Jacob Getzels, an American psychologist, proposed that there is a second stage in which the chaos of ideas and knowledge incubate the work, and that this requires gathering and remembering as well as letting go and forgetting. Most psychologists agree that the ability to make connections is a vital part of the process. Fromm says that all humans desire to be creative and, by doing so, to transcend. Recent work by Mihaly Csikszentmihalyi on a concept he calls 'flow' would seem to corroborate this. Flow, according to Csikszentmihalyi, is a concentration that transcends the difficulties of daily existence and brings inner contentment. Perhaps this feeling of flow is why so many people find writing such a satisfying activity, regardless of whether there is a published product at the end of the process.

Writers would do well to investigate and understand their process: know what turns you on as a writer, and then work with this. Try music, try walking, try pencils and paper if you are a dedicated laptop user: sometimes a subtle shift in method can kick-start a weary creative process.

It helps when you know that the initial difficulties with a work are only a phase you're going through, and that if you keep working you will make it through to the other side. It is possible that some instances of writer's block are examples of writers who refuse an aspect of the process because it seems insurmountably difficult, but remember the oft-quoted words: there's no gain without pain. So identify the things about writing you find difficult and turn to face them. Make yourself finish something, even if it feels like pulling teeth; and remember that not all writing activity can be about wild and fiery inspiration; sometimes there is sweat and slog and boredom as you battle through the necessary bits that need writing to hold together the parts written in light. _HN_

Writing idea

Archaeology
Remember the last piece of creative writing you completed. Where did the idea come from? Which parts did you write first? Which parts did you really enjoy writing? Which parts were a drag to write? Where did you write best? Keep a commentary journal in which to write _about_ your writing. You'll slowly build a picture of your process, and by knowing what best suits your writing process and what hinders it, you'll be able to seek out your more successful writing behaviours and replicate them in the process of writing the next piece you work on.

Further reading

Fromm, Erich in Harold Anderson (ed.), _Creativity and its Cultivation_ (New York: Harper & Row, 1959).

creativity

Mental output which requires input: creative people feed their minds with beautiful art, colours, music; they expose themselves to new ideas, new facts, poetry, current affairs, vivid landscapes and strange and interesting experiences. Researchers investigating the traits of creative people tend to agree that they are receptive and divergent thinkers: that is to say, they have open minds and they make unexpected links between seemingly disparate ideas: they can, for example, list hundreds of uses for a brick. Researchers also agree that creativity is enhanced by being immersed in a subject. It can be fired up by talking to other creative people who jolt your thought patterns into new and unexpected places, and it doesn't give up at the first sign of a problem: creativity often meets seemingly insurmountable blocks which lift when something is subtly changed. Many writers advocate taking a short walk; others recommend sleeping on a problem and allowing the subconscious mind to set to work.   *HN*

Further reading
Csikszentmihalyi, Milhaly, *Creativity: Flow and the Psychology of Discovery and Invention* (London: HarperCollins, 1996).
Goldberg, Natalie, *Wild Mind: Living the Writer's Life* (London: Rider, 1991).

crime
What is it that makes crime one of the most popular subjects for fiction? There are plenty of theories, the most obvious being that even the most law-abiding of us are beasts beneath the civilized veneer, that we need a vicarious space to play at being bad. Another is that crime fiction is structured in the form of a narrative puzzle, offering a neat and satisfying solution, unlike life, which mostly remains unsolved. Look for plot ideas in the newspapers, current and archived; research police and criminal justice methods to ensure accuracy; and get into the mind of your characters: both baddies and goodies. Don't make the solution obvious but don't make it gratuitous either. Read Henning Mankell, Sara Paretsky and Ian Rankin to see how well it can be done.   *HL*

data

Information that enhances the quality of your writing. In fiction or in a screenplay, you are trying to build a believable world in the mind of the reader. Each detail you can specify within that picture becomes a little jewel that decorates the fabric and enhances the imagined world. This will often involve the sort of research a reporter engages in: going to the trouble of acquiring information about your subject, be it cosmetics or rugby league, so that your work will have texture and be credible. The research you undertake may be so that you can present your characters in their workplaces convincingly, or it may be to bring a setting alive – Greenland or a fashionable club.   *RG*

(See also **research**)

daydreaming

When exterior stimuli fail to draw and maintain attention, the mind is more available to the self-generated images drifting through. While in schools and workplaces this is not considered desirable, for the health of their craft, writers should (re)learn to pay more attention to the internal kaleidoscope of ideas and images. Music can assist: try The Boards of Canada; Loscil; Brian Eno; Aphex Twin's *Selected Ambient Works Vol. II*. Put on some headphones, find that not-quite-awake, not-quite-asleep state of mind, and write as you dream. Enjoy.   *HN*

Death of the Author, The

The title of an essay by the French literary critic and theorist, Roland Barthes, which is much misunderstood. When badly taught on Eng. Lit. courses, this idea may be read as the triumph of the critic and reader over the writer, not a cheery theory for those of us struggling to be authors ourselves. However, Barthes did not mean that there were no such persons as Shakespeare or Stephen King. He meant (put simply) that writing is not owned and controlled by an all-powerful author but comes out of the complex interaction between the individual writer and the particular mesh of language, time and culture they are part of. A book is also read differently in different contexts. This is not to deny that there was once an original intention and creation, but to assert that it is futile to search for one absolute interpretation, for 'what the author really meant'. All texts, all writings and readings are varied and changing. If you observe what actually happens when you are writing and reading, you will find that Barthes wasn't as daft as his theory sounds.   *HL*

Further reading

Barthes, Roland (ed. and trans. Stephen Heath), 'The Death of the Author', in *Image–Music–Text* (New York: Hill, 1977).

description

How writers render the worlds they create. There are two schools of thought on how to work with description. One favours lush, lavish prose; in the other, less description is always more. The likelihood is that in your writing you will at different times subscribe to both schools of thought. The latter, more minimalist approach was that favoured by modernist writers and goes back to Chekhov. In prose description, Chekhov contended, you need to leave the reader room to work, as a working reader is a happy reader (see **clutter**). Readers only have time to glance at your descriptions of character, action and setting. This is not just because they are in a hurry; it is also because at any given time in narrative writing readers are being asked to give their attention to several elements at once – things such as what characters are saying and doing or the setting. If your description of any of these elements is thick with detail – cluttered – readers will neither be able to absorb what you say nor know which details are important and which not. In description of the kind Chekhov promoted, clarity, simplicity and economy are of the essence. For this reason, it's good to conflate wherever possible. One area where this is very possible is in verb and adverb combinations. If you can, replace a verb and adverb with a simple verb that means the same thing. For example, *She hit him hard* might easily become *She walloped him*, which is more direct, and directness in description is essential. You don't want your reader stopping and wondering what you meant.

It's all very well saying that less is more, but how do you know whether you have included enough or too much? As Ursula Hurley indicates here, knowing is always a judgement call:

The art is in judging what is salient and what is boring, when to zoom in and when to draw back, when to show and when to leave intriguing gaps, when to elongate and when to contract. (Hurley, 2006, p. 175)

The late Brian Moore, who in a distinguished career delivered umpteen novels, most of which weighed in at around 200 pages – not many like him now – includes enough but not too much description as he sets up a religious ceremony here:

Priests, nuns, students and dignitaries, all were mulatto or black. On the wall behind the microphones and the podium was a large photograph of our new Pope, himself a man of mixed blood. And then, walking past the podium, a ghost from the past, this stooped white man in a frayed cassock, incongruous as the blackamoor attendant in a sixteenth-century painting of the French court. (Moore, 1995, pp. 1–2)

However, in my opinion – and I can't see the author's reputation being damaged by *that* – John Updike includes a good deal too much description here:

Along Prospect Street, the shadows of the half-abandoned houses extended from curb to curb, although in the sky overhead racing white clouds and negative patches of stark blue still spoke of bright day. At the rear of the vacant lot stood a marvel I had not noticed when walking this way thirty minutes ago: a shapely tall gingko tree, each of its shuddering fan-shaped leaves turned, with a uniformity unlike the ragged turning of the less primordial deciduous trees, a plangent yellow monotone. The tree seemed a towering outcry there in this derelict block, in a passing slash of sun. (Updike, 1986, pp. 73–4)

Without dismantling this passage piece by piece, my view is that there is too much detail here for the reader to take in. I can't help wondering if the gingko tree is necessary, let alone its comparison with other trees. How you know the difference between enough and too much is a matter of taste. But it may help to ask why you have included the detail you have. In the Brian Moore passage, the detail creates the setting for the opening chapter. In the John Updike, the detail also informs the setting, but since the action of the chapter is over, you have to ask if this derelict block is a necessary part of the novel's setting.

description

Any narrative-based writing – whether fiction, memoir or script – is much more like a moving picture than a photograph. A photograph – a still, if you like – involves static description, which does exactly what it says on the tin. When your description is static, your story has stopped. When your story stops, your reader disengages. A story should always be moving forward, so it makes sense to deliver description on the hoof. This is done by incorporating it into the action and dialogue, as Anita Shreve does here in this passage from *Light on Snow*:

> We turn a corner and see a small room in which a half-dozen people sit on plastic chairs attached to the walls. A woman in jeans is pacing, her yellow hair still bearing the imprint of her rollers. She seems impatient, annoyed with a sullen boy who might be her son. He sits in his plastic chair, his coat still on, his chin besieged by angry pimples. I think I see the reason for the visit in the way he cradles his right hand: a finger? A wrist? My father walks toward the Triage window and stands at its opening while a woman speaking into a telephone ignores him. (Shreve, 2005, p. 12)

The half-dozen people are introduced while the narrator is turning a corner. The woman's hair is described as she is pacing. The sullen boy is bundled with her annoyance and the final sentence includes new information and action on the part of the father and the woman on the phone. At any one of these points, Shreve could have stopped and given us a full description – of the room, the woman, the boy, the father, the woman at the window. Because she didn't, we find it easy to keep reading.

In the other school of thought about description, economy and concision are less favoured than lush detail and sharply honed elaboration. Take a look at this passage from Ian McEwan's novel *Atonement*:

> Some miles beyond the Tallises' land rose the Surrey Hills and their motionless crowds of thick crested oaks, their greens softened by a milky heat haze. Then, nearer, the estate's open parkland, which today had a dry and savage look, roasting like a savannah, where isolated trees threw harsh stumpy shadows and the long grass was already stalked by the leonine yellow of high summer. (McEwan, 2001, p. 38)

Here phrase is layered upon phrase, and there appears to have been an attempt to describe the landscape comprehensively. It still works, though, if in a rather ornate way.

Sometimes you will go beyond the lean cadences of concision in order to be more lyrical, to be a little effusive about a character's emotions, or to introduce a musical quality to your description. Creating musical prose is about descriptive writing, but there are other ingredients beyond descriptive prose. This kind of lyrical writing has to do with sculpting and shaping your words and clauses so that they are more beautiful than their function demands. It's also about having a love for words, for their sounds as much as their meaning. You may see what I mean in William Faulkner's use of poetic devices such as sibilance, consonance and alliteration in this extract from 'That Evening Sun':

> The streets are paved now, and the telephone and electric companies are cutting down more and more of the shade trees – the water oaks, the maples and locusts and elms – to make room for iron poles bearing clusters of bloated and ghostly grapes, and we have a city laundry which makes the rounds on Monday morning, gathering bundles of clothes into bright-coloured, specially made motorcars: the soiled wearing of a whole week now flees apparitionlike behind alert and irritable electric horns, with a diminishing noise of rubber and asphalt like tearing silk, and even the Negro women who still take in white people's washing after the old custom, fetch and deliver it in auto-mobiles. (Faulkner, 1991, p. 51)

Lastly, a word about turning the heat up on your description: look out for weak intensifiers in your work. A weak intensifier is an adjective designed to convey something more strongly that ends up conveying it more weakly. An extreme example could be something like this: *The dog was totally dead.* Does 'totally' make the dog seem more dead? Much more effective is the simple *The dog was dead.*   RG

Writing ideas

1. *De-cluttering*

   Find a first draft of a piece of your writing, one that includes some description. Bearing in mind Chekhov's advice (see **clutter**), go through this draft and remove all the clutter so that a reader will, as Chekhov puts it, understand it at once.

2. *Describing on the hoof*

   Write a scene which involves an accident of some kind in which one of the characters is hurt. The one stipulation is that all description must be incorporated into action or dialogue – no stopping the story to describe anything.

Further reading

Faulkner, William, *Selected Stories* (London: Penguin, 1991).

Hurley, Ursula, in 'Description' in Graham et al., *How To Write Fiction (And Think About It)* (Basingstoke: Palgrave, 2006).

McEwan, Ian, *Atonement* (London: Jonathan Cape, 2001).

Moore, Brian, *No Other Life* (London: Flamingo, 1995), pp. 1–2.

Shreve, Anita, *Light on Snow* (London: Abacus, 2005), p. 12.

Updike, John, *Roger's Version* (London: Penguin Group, 1986), pp. 73–4.

desk

You don't need a desk. Jane Austen is said to have written at the kitchen table, ready to help with the household tasks at any moment, which is probably a myth. Stephen King says he wrote his first two novels on a child's desk balanced on his thighs. Roald Dahl, in his later years, sat in an old chair with a rug over his knees. Most people, however, need a flat surface for a word processor and space to spread out a little. It doesn't matter whether it's tidy but it's good to have a dictionary and thesaurus nearby and somewhere to put your coffee cup. Desks can become fetishistic: perhaps focusing on place and object helps us to deal with not knowing exactly how writing happens.   *HL*

(See **room**)

Further reading

Krementz, Jill, *The Writer's Desk* (London: Random House, 1997).

detail

The little things that count. It's important to get detail right. Not just any old detail, though. Telling detail – detail, to spell it out, that tells you something significant about character, setting or situation – is what you're after. Details are a significant tool in your attempts to create something mimetic, something like life. John Gardner speaks of 'authenticating detail'. 'The reader', he argues, 'is regularly presented with proofs – in the form of closely observed details – that what is said to be happening is really happening' (Gardner, 1999, p. 26). There are many physical details I could give you about my late uncle, but if I put him in a piece of fiction and only mentioned his glass eye, always looking off to one side, and the fact that his left thumb was always grimy from tamping down the ash in his pipe, he would probably come alive to you.

Always get the detail right. If I wrote that *apfelstrudel* is one of the staples of Australian cuisine, your confidence in my authority would be terminally undermined. Getting the details right makes your work convincing and doing so will often involve research.   *RG*

(See also **description**)

dialect

Dialect is a characteristic form of language used by people from a particular geographical region. Technically, dialect refers only to grammar and vocabulary, whereas accent refers to pronunciation, although the two are inextricably linked. Where I come from, in the north of England, for example, the children's chasing game is called *ticky-it*, not *tag* or *it*, as it is in other areas, and some people say *them* instead of *those*, as in *Give me them apples, please.*

In the UK, we also have an 'official' dialect called Received Pronunciation, RP, sometimes called BBC English, which is often taught at school as correct English, thus creating a hierarchy which relegates other dialects as lower class. To counteract this, some writers use dialect in their work partly as a challenge to the perceived cultural imperialism of RP. See, in particular, contemporary Scottish writers, such as Liz Lochhead and Tom Leonard, as well as writers of Afro-Caribbean origin, for particular examples.

Until relatively recently, dialect has primarily meant variation in language use *within* a particular country or geographical locality. However, with the growth of English as an international language, dialect is better understood as relating to world Englishes (see also **English**). Standard written English will serve most purposes, but the fiction writer needs to be aware that there are many variations. American and British Englishes, for example, have many alternative words, idioms and expressions, which, if you get them wrong, can leave you looking as if you don't know your maths from your math, your chips from your crisps, or your arse from your ass. If your characters use a different local or international English dialect from your own, you may need research to create authentic speech.

In the UK, we are culturally attuned, helped along by Shakespeare and the British class system, to stigmatize or laugh at people who talk differently from us. However, spoken and written speech are different animals and *everybody's* speech when written phonetically will appear to be a kind of dialect. Most people, for example, miss off word endings, as in *I'm goin out*. The challenge for writers is how to translate the richness of speech into text without patronizing or marginalization. *HL*

dialogue

What characters in fiction say to one another – and just as fictional characters aren't entirely like real people, fictional dialogue isn't entirely like real speech. Real conversation is unedited and contains much that is dull. The trick with writing dialogue, according to John Singleton, is 'making the artificial and crafted appear natural and unforced; hiding the art in artlessness' (Singleton, in Graham et al., 2005, p. 156).

When we speak, most of what we communicate is at a non-verbal level. Clearly characters on a printed page do not have the option of non-verbal communication, nor can they have tone of voice. If we were in each other's presence, I could say to you 'I'm really looking forward to this' and convey unequivocally that I was not looking forward to it at all. So the first thing to learn about dialogue is that it is much more than recording the things real people say. At one level, you are recording less than all of what real people might say. At another level, this may require you to suggest more than what is said – to ensure that the reader understands when one thing is said and another thing is meant. Dialogue in fiction is artful, edited, crafted and shaped to achieve many purposes.

Good dialogue is a means of creating **immediacy** in fiction. It shows things as they happen; it shows the story's reality unfolding. As you give your characters words, they come to life. Indirect speech is a news report of what happened, but direct speech – dialogue – is a live broadcast of what happened. Compare these two brief extracts from Yann Martell's *Life of Pi*. The first is interior monologue, the narrator Pi addressing the reader:

I owe to Hinduism the original landscape of my religious imagination, those towns and rivers, battlefields and forests, holy mountains and deep seas where gods, saints, villains and ordinary people rub shoulders, and, in doing so, define who and why we are. (Martell, 2002, p. 50)

The second is direct speech:

> 'Where are you?' I asked.
> 'I'm here,' he replied wearily.
> 'But where is that? I can't see you.'
> 'Why can't you see me?'
> 'I've gone blind.'
> 'What?' he exclaimed. (Martell, 2002, p. 249)

Which is more immediate? Which is more dramatic? And which more engaging? It's obvious that the second extract is a scene. Fiction depends on scenes – I would question whether a piece of fiction without any scenes is indeed fiction – and the appearance of dialogue is the most obvious signal to the reader that a scene has begun. In short, dialogue is an inimitable way of bringing your fiction alive.

Good dialogue is taut and creates narrative tension, as you will see in this extract from John McGahern's *Amongst Women*:

> 'That salt,' Moran demanded.
> 'What salt?'
> 'Are there two salts? Pass the salt!'
> Instead of lifting the small cruet, Michael pushed it across the table towards his father. Moran seethed as he watched. As it was pushed, the small glass cruet touched a fold in the tablecloth and overturned.
> 'You wouldn't pass salt that way to a dog.' Moran rose from the table. 'Have you any idea who you are passing salt to?'
> 'I didn't mean for it to overturn.' Michael was at an intolerable disadvantage sitting down.
> 'You just shoved it over to the dog.'
> 'I tell you I didn't mean . . .'
> 'I'll teach you to mean something!' Moran struck him violently but he managed partly to avert the blow, the chair falling over as he jumped to his feet. (McGahern, 1990, pp. 119–20)

Here each speech adds to the tension of the previous one. If you want to see how, exactly, you could go through the passage and replace responses which are aggressive and add to the conflict with ones which are passive and reduce the level of conflict. Note also that the two characters use brief speeches and short sentences, both of which help to generate the sense of tension that is generated by what they actually say.

Dialogue reveals character. We find out about characters in fiction most effectively through what they say and what they do. A corollary of this is that each line of every speech ought to be so characteristic of the speaker that no other character could possibly have said it. Here, in an extract from Jonathan Coe's *The Closed Circle*, two old schoolfriends are catching up:

Benjamin hesitated for a moment, then leaned forward. 'There is someone,' he confided. 'She works quite near our house. She's a hair-dresser.'

'A hairdresser?'

'Yes. She's gorgeous. She has this really . . . angelic face. Angelic and sophisticated at the same time.'

'And how old is she?'

'I don't know – late twenties, maybe, something like that.'

'Name?'

'I don't know. I haven't actually – '

' – spoken to her,' said Claire, finishing off his sentence with the weariest of inflections. 'Christ, Benjamin, what are you *like*? You're in your forties for fuck's sake – '

'Only just.'

'And you've got a crush on a hairdresser who you've never spoken to? This is who you're seriously considering as your future life partner?' (Coe, 2004, p. 215)

Even if you hadn't read the couple of hundred pages preceding this passage, you could probably tell that Benjamin is a romantic, sensitive bumbler whose character is largely presented in a comic way. You could probably also tell that Claire is feisty and forthright, with a tendency to be fiery. They are character-ized by what they say. Also, you should note that it would be difficult to swap their speeches over, giving Claire's to Benjamin and vice versa. To do so would entirely alter their characters. Dialogue is always characteristic of the speaker.

Good dialogue is often indirect. As in life, characters say one thing and mean another. In terms of narrative engagement, this is very helpful because it causes readers to do some work – to deduce what it is the character really means. Making the reader work is always desirable, because an active reader is an engaged reader. In Ann Beattie's story 'A Vintage Thunderbird', the eponymous car comes to represent the relationship between Nick and Karen. The story ends with her selling the car. This speech, we clearly understand, is not about the selling of the car – it's about whether or not the relationship is finished.

> 'I just want to ask one thing,' he said, 'and then I'll never mention it again. Are you sure the deal is final?' (Beattie, 1991, p. 20)

Dialogue consists of what is said – the speech – and, possibly, a speech tag (for example, 'he said'). If at all possible, it's a good idea to lose the speech tag. Why? Because the speech is the part you want the reader to notice. For this reason, an exotic speech tag ('she expostulated') is a bad idea. (Which will stand out more: what's said or 'she expostulated'?) You may also be tempted to describe how the speech has been said. Don't. The necessary adverb will only add more clutter and distraction and, as the novelist Penelope Fitzgerald admits:

> When I'm writing myself I have a slight sense of failure every time I put in a 'sharply' or a 'reluctantly'. The characters and the situation between them ought to have made it clear how sharp, or how reluctant they are. (Fitzgerald, in Boylan, 1993, p. 143)

Of course, omitting speech tag adverbs leaves the readers to work out for themselves how things have been said, and you already know that this is what you want.

Finally, a word about balance: how much dialogue should your fiction contain? There are those writers whose work contains a very high proportion of dialogue – Roddy Doyle and Haruki Murakami, for example – and those who include very little – Jonathan Swift and Alice McDermott – but my advice is that too much dialogue will tend to make your fiction feel insubstantial. If you check through some of the novels on your shelves, I think you will find that most contemporary fiction includes a balance between dialogue and narrative passages.   *RG*

Writing ideas
1. *Speaking tension*
   Write a page of dialogue with two characters speaking, one of whom increases the tension with each thing he or she says – as Moran does in the John McGahern passage above.

2. *Showing tone*

   Penelope Fitzgerald writes of her sense of failure if she has to describe the way something is said. Write a page of dialogue in which you attach an adverb and a speech tag to every speech. Then go back and remove all the adverbs and, if necessary, adapt what the characters say so that *how* they say it is apparent. Also, for discipline, remove all the speech tags that you can manage without.

3. *Characteristic dialogue*

   Take a piece of dialogue from something you have been working on and check that each speech could only have been said by the person speaking. If anything doesn't sound characteristic of the speaker, alter it so that it does.

Further reading

Beattie, Ann, 'A Vintage Thunderbird', in *Secrets & Surprises* (New York: Vintage, 1991).

Coe, Jonathan, *The Closed Circle* (London: Viking, 2004).

Fitzgerald, Penelope ,'Hearing Them Speak', in Clare Boylan (ed.), *The Agony and the Ego* (London: Penguin, 1993).

Graham, Robert, Helen Newall, Heather Leach and John Singleton (eds), *The Road To Somewhere: A Creative Writing Companion* (Basingstoke: Palgrave, 2005).

McGahern, John, *Amongst Women* (London: Faber, 1990).

Martell, Yann, *Life of Pi* (London: Canongate, 2002).

digression

Letting the writing digress, without forcing or censoring, is a good way to find a story, and writers who are stuck in the middle may need to allow themselves to get a little bit lost in order to find out what it is they want to say. Virginia Woolf called this 'feathering about'. A temporary turn from the main narrative drag onto an interesting side road can be particularly useful as **breathing space** after dramatic events. 'Digressions . . . are the sunshine; they are the life, the soul of reading', said Laurence Sterne, whose novel *Tristram Shandy* was all digression.   HL

Further reading

Sterne, Laurence, *The Life and Opinions of Tristram Shandy, Gentleman* (London: Penguin, 2002).

directness

The information you wish the reader to understand should travel as directly as possible from your mind to the reader's. To write with greater directness, you need first to eliminate **clutter**. The use of active **verbs** rather than passive ones will also help. Finally, avoid qualifying clauses. *The cat sat on the mat* is much more direct and efficient than *The cat sat on the mat – well, to be honest, it was more a case of perching than sitting.* Get it right first time then move along.   *RG*

displacement activities

The many and various things you do when you know you should be settling down to write: making a cup of tea; tidying your desk; tidying the kitchen; filling the washing machine; emptying the washing machine; playing The Sims; doing more research; lying down with the cat to reduce blood pressure. The first step in fighting displacement activities is identifying them. Once you know that you are diverting yourself from the work you are meant to be doing, it may be easier to get back to it. As with fear of the blank screen, a problem with displacement activities may be helped by being in a regular writing routine.   *RG*

double-spacing

Text formatting that contains a full blank line between each of the lines. It makes your manuscript more readable and is essential when submitting work for discussion or publication. Workshop members, agents, editors and proof-readers need plenty of space in which to make marks and comments. Many word-processing programs have text spacing set as single space by default – to change this in Microsoft Word select the text then press and hold the Ctrl key and press 2.   *HL*

drafts

Versions of a piece of writing. In an interview in *Paris Review*, Hemingway said he'd rewritten the ending of *A Farewell to Arms* 44 times. Asked what the problem was, he said, 'Getting the words right.' Yesterday on the radio, I heard Ali Smith say that her novels take her two to four years to complete. Her novels are not long. If you are going to be a writer, you are going to have to get used to the fact that each piece of work you produce will go through a number of – possibly a lot of – drafts. It has been said that good novels are not written, they are rewritten.   *RG*

drama

'Life with the dull bits cut out', according to Alfred Hitchcock. So yes, drama is about the momentous, not the domestic. That's true, but it's also true that many classic narratives are domestic and that it's limiting to think that unless a death is involved, a story is not dramatic. Drama has to do with suspense and intrigue and is generated by conflict. Putting your characters in peril is one way of creating drama. There has to be something at stake. The reader needs to be wondering if Rocky can really overcome his disadvantages to become world champion, or if Oliver is going to spend the rest of his days in Fagin's evil clutches.

RG

dramatization

Rendering a story so that it is recreated for the reader, or amplifying situations so that they engage the reader. Fiction is a dramatized imitation of real life. In dramatizing, you are, if you like, re-presenting your story material. The opposite of dramatizing is relating or recounting a story, telling the reader about what happened. Readers don't want to hear about what happened; they want to experience it for themselves. Explanation, too, is the opposite of dramatization. Readers will barely take on board what you tell them, but they will experience vicariously what you dramatize. Writing about the work of Henry James, Percy Lubbock said:

> The art of fiction does not begin until the novelist thinks of his story as a matter to be shown, to be so exhibited that it will tell itself. (Hall, 1989, p. 2)

What we are talking about, in other words, is showing rather than telling. Think about that imitation of life, about the idea of recreating your dramatic material for the reader to experience. Another helpful angle on dramatizing is that you are putting your characters and their situations onstage for the reader to witness. In dramatizing, you will not be telling readers about what happens; instead you will be using your craft to create a drama in their heads.

At the centre of showing is action and dialogue. A good writer, according to John Gardner,

> can get anything at all across through action and dialogue, and if he can think of no powerful reason to do otherwise, he should probably leave explanation to his reviewers and critics. (Gardner, 1991, p. 111)

As your characters act and speak, the story unfolds and your reader experiences it as it happens. One productive step towards successful showing is to concentrate on these two elements – the action and the dialogue. Showing is designed to give your readers an immediate experience (see also **immediacy**), so removing all that is extraneous from your fiction will maximize this: clutter, qualifying phrases, explanation, asides, redundancies, the presence of the author.

Showing should make detectives of your readers. They see that one of the characters bites her nails extensively when another is talking about a robbery at the local newsagent's. The reader can deduce that the nail-biter knows something about the robbery. Look at it this way: when you watch a film, nobody stands at the side of the screen explaining what's going on, telling you what to watch out for. You notice what you notice and make your own deductions. Showing in fiction both gives readers what they need to do this – actions, dialogue, gestures, facial expressions – and leaves them alone to do it.

Telling, the opposite of showing, often occurs in fiction when you decide to give the reader important information on a plate. Readers don't want information on a plate, though; they want it in a scene, dramatized. Telling in its purest form is **exposition**, background information presented to the reader by the author. Exposition is often in the pluperfect tense, the 'had been' tense. In terms of creating a sense of immediacy for your readers, the pluperfect tense could not be more wrong for the job. It is to immediacy what a cheeseburger is to healthy eating.

In any novel, however, telling is a valid mode. The problem for the writer is knowing when to use it, and the answer, I think, is not to tell readers about episodes that are dramatically significant. The readers want to be present for the key moments in any narrative, so these ought not to be recounted or related but need to happen on stage. Thus, most of the time the writer ought to be working hard at making readers feel that they are in the story, with all their senses working overtime to help them experience first-hand what the characters are experiencing. *RG*

Writing ideas
1. Using a piece of fiction you have already written, find three things you have told the reader and show them instead, in scenes – however short – made up of action and dialogue.
2. Dig out a novel by your favourite writer. Read the first chapter, marking

the passages that are told and those that are shown. Now, in writing, see if you can work out why the author decided which should be told and which shown. Would you have done it the same way?

Further reading

Gardner, John, *The Art of Fiction: Notes on Craft for Young Writers* (New York: Vintage, 1991), p. 111.
Hall, Oakley, *The Art and Craft of Fiction* (Cincinnati: Story Press, 1989).

dreams

Whether or not they are the omens they were once supposed to be, Freud and Jung certainly considered them access to what goes on beneath the conscious mind. Since dreams are often strange and bewildering, writers sometimes use them as plot devices to shift a protagonist's (metaphorical or otherwise) journey. This might not be so far from the truth since there are accounts of scientists dreaming solutions to otherwise baffling problems: Friedrich Kekulé is supposed to have understood the composition of benzene in a dream. So keep a dream diary. And, as Kekulé said: let us learn to dream, gentlemen. *HN*

eavesdropping

The best writers are those who have clearly spent their lives studying other people. Part of this is **observation** but eavesdropping has a significant role to play, too. Tuning in to what people say on trains, at bus stops or in the staff room is not only fun but also a very valuable discipline for writers. (But no amount of eavesdropping will do you any good unless you record it in your **notebook**.) My favourite kind of eavesdropping is sitting in cafés. Why? Mainly because it's possible to have your notebook open and write down what you hear as you hear it. Not so easy at a bus stop.   *RG*

e-books

Many IT experts and cultural commentators believe that it will only be a matter of time before the conventional book is displaced by an electronic form. The codex book is such a familiar object with its paper pages stitched or glued together and bound inside covers, that we take it for granted as an essential part of our world. However, there are a number of people who argue (some with dread and some with relish) that computers – in particular the internet – may soon send the book the way of the papyrus scroll. Jay David Bolter argues that

> The printed book seems destined to move to the margin of our literate culture . . . electronic technology offers us a new kind of book and new ways to read and write. (Bolter, 1991, p. 2)

Bolter points out that online writing and publishing will tend to turn readers into writers and, although he was speaking in the early 1990s – ancient history in internet terms – his predictions appear to be accurate, as can be seen by the enormous proliferation of personal websites, online diaries, **blogs**, etc., all made possible by the internet, which means that anybody can publish their own work and have direct access to a world of readers.

The expectation is that all books will eventually become accessible and downloadable onto computer or handheld device. Pages will be 'turned' by pressing a key and there could be added bells and whistles like interactivity and multimedia. In September 2006, Ebooks.com was advertising 69,000 e-books which could be downloaded, and almost certainly such enterprises will expand and mature. E-books and journals *have* proliferated throughout the web, particularly for educational use, but most are still printed out rather than read from a screen, and the confusing proliferation of handheld devices, some with incompatible operating systems, alienates many people. So far the e-book revolution hasn't happened in the way that picture, video and music downloads have, but it does seem inevitable that many people will one day buy or borrow texts from an online resource which can be directly downloaded onto an electronic reading device. Fears that conventional printed books are about to disappear may be premature but these developments are clearly relevant to all writers. Watch this space.   *HL*

Further reading
Bolter, D. J., *Writing Space* (London: Laurence Erlbaum Associates, 1991).
E-books at www.ebooks.com.

editing

Pruning, proofreading, refining. 'Every word is there for a reason, and if not, I cross it out', the novelist Jerzy Kosinski wrote. Even good material must sometimes go: 'Murder your darlings', G. K. Chesterton advised. Some of what you do when editing is this kind of weeding out of the superfluous. Proofreading is another one of the chores involved – eliminating typos and grammatical errors. You might also look for and remove any redundancies or ambiguities. You might sometimes find that you have not used the *mot précis* – was the experience 'horrid' or 'horrendous'? Sometimes editing will mean re-ordering your material – for instance, moving the information that Ben is diabetic earlier in the narrative because readers need to be primed with it. *RG*

editor

After (or alongside) your agent, the single most important person in your literary life. They vary in seniority within the publishing firm they work for and will give you every kind of necessary advice on the triumphs and failings of your work. Remember, the editor is building a career just as much as the writer and it is they who have to fight your corner when it comes to buying the book and marketing it. They need as much ammunition as you can give them.

A good editor will require you to redraft the book they have bought and will give you advice as to the direction your future writing should take. You will also be subject to the textual intervention of a copy-editor to ensure accurate spelling, grammar, continuity and conformity to house style.

In *Rotten Rejections* (ed. André Bernard, London: Robson Books, 1991), the illustrious John Gardner says of editors:

> One should fight like the devil the temptation to think well of editors. They are all, without exception – at least some of the time – incompetent or crazy. By the nature of their profession they read too much, with the result they grow jaded and cannot recognise talent though it dances in front of their eyes.

GC

email

If you're looking for ways to make your fiction more various, using emails is a neat narrative strategy. Emails have the advantages of the **epistolary** form, but are generally more succinct than letters. Many writers have used e-mail exchanges in their fiction, but if you want to see it well handled, take a look at Jonathan Coe's *The Closed Circle*.

In terms of the real thing, there's a certain danger involved. For people who write, email is perhaps a more appealing way to communicate than texting. However, there's always a risk, especially if emailing is central to your work, that you will spend too much time writing emails and not enough time producing your own writing. RG

emotion

In your readers, a priority. 'Thought-provoking' is all very well, but if readers find what you write emotive, it's altogether more desirable. Remember, though, that this means moving your readers, not depressing them. Reaching for novels from my shelves at random, I find reviews using words such as 'captivating', 'funny', 'heartbreaking' and 'beguiling'. If you involve readers' emotions you are getting something right – something important. How you do it begins with making readers care about your characters. Once they care about them, any jeopardy you throw at your characters is going to engage readers' emotions more deeply. RG

endings

T. S. Eliot said 'the end is where we start from' ('Little Gidding', Part V) and although he was speaking about life in general, this may be helpful advice for the fiction writer. If you know where your story is heading, then you have something to work towards, a fixed point of reference to keep you on track. On the other hand, you may be the kind of writer who prefers to work it out as you go along. Some, particularly those who challenge literary convention, argue that pre-ordained endings are false and formulaic. André Gide commented that

> Life never presents us with anything which may not be looked upon as a fresh starting point . . . 'Might be continued' – these are the words with which I should like to finish. (Gide, in Allott, 1959, p. 251)

But stories are not life. As Gide implies, life is messy and inconclusive whereas fiction rounds things off and ties up the loose ends. One of the reasons we love conventional stories is *because* they are conclusive. They offer a vision of the world where the detective always solves the crime, the killer is always brought to justice and order is restored. In the last scene of Shakespeare's *Romeo and Juliet*, after their deaths, the Prince speaks the final authoritative words: 'See, what a scourge is laid upon your hate . . . all are punish'd', and although the young lovers lie dead, their death has a tragic inevitability that ultimately satisfies: a lesson has been learned and life can move on, everyone all the wiser.

You can plan for endings or you can wait for the ending to reveal itself to you as you write. You can even give a story more than one ending, as John Fowles did in *The French Lieutenant's Woman*; there are no absolute rules and we all have to find our own best way. However, there doesn't need to be a dramatic ending of the 'all lie dead' or 'lived happily ever after' type. For instance, a story may end when we have reached the heart of a character. In Alice Munro's *Runaway*, on the next to last page, one of the main characters, Carla, discovers something terrible about her husband. But she is not quite sure what it means:

> Carla found she had got used to the sharp thought that had lodged in her. It wasn't so sharp anymore . . . She had only to raise her eyes, to look in one direction to know where she might go. An evening walk, once her chores for the day were finished. To the edge of the woods

where the buzzards had held their party. And then the dirty little bones in the grass. Or perhaps not. Nothing there. Other things could have happened . . . (Munro, 2006, p. 47)

Munro doesn't let Carla come to a resolution so it is the *reader* who sees the danger, while Carla prevaricates: 'she had got used . . . or perhaps not . . . other things could have . . .' At the end of *Runaway*, we see what the story has been subtly showing us all along about Carla's character. Like all good endings, this one shines a light backwards through the narrative, illuminating what was there all the time. *HL*

Writing ideas
Here are three possible conclusions:

* 'It lay there at his feet, silent and unmoving, the blood trickling from its body. There was no doubt this time. It was finally, completely, dead.'
* 'He walked towards her smiling, his hands outstretched.'
* 'As night fell, I opened the door and, closing it quietly behind me, walked away for the last time.'

Choose one then write a story towards it. You can use one of the above or make up your own.

Further reading
Allott, Miriam, *Novelists on the Novel* (London: Routledge, 1965).
Eliot, T. S., *Four Quartets* (London: Faber, 2001).
Fowles, John, *The French Lieutenant's Woman* (London: Vintage, 2004).
Munro, Alice, *Runaway* (London: Vintage, 2006).

English
In 1603, the year of the first Queen Elizabeth's death, it is estimated that there were between 3 and 7 million English speakers in the world, most of them living within the British Isles. By 1952, when Queen Elizabeth II came to the throne, the estimated numbers had risen to 250 million. At the beginning of the twenty-first century it was thought that almost 400 million used English as a first language and over 1,000 million used at least some English regularly. Modern English may have begun in a small island on the edge of Europe but it is now a world language with as many forms of English

as there are peoples who speak it: Caribbean English; Singapore English; Indian English; Nigerian English; Black English Vernacular; Irish English; Scottish English; these are just a few examples. (See *The Cambridge Encyclopedia of the English Language* by David Crystal.)

This rapid and increasing spread is mainly due to political and economic factors, beginning with the founding of the American colonies in the sixteenth century and continuing with British and American imperial expansion during the eighteenth and nineteenth centuries. Today, globalization, emigration and the internet drive the advance at an even greater rate.

Some people argue that the expansion of English is a threat, a continuation of the colonial process, invading, diluting, and sometimes even killing off other languages, as in the case of Irish and a range of Australian Aboriginal languages. France, fearing that the French language is being undermined, has even gone so far as to legislate against the use of English words in certain official documents.

The expansion of English has great significance for the writer, particularly for those who are not English by birth or original culture. Ngugi wa Thiong'o, a Kenyan novelist who began writing in English, now writes only in his native language, Gikuyu, arguing that, for him, English in Africa is a 'cultural bomb' (Thiong'o, 1981, p. 15). On the other hand, there are many post-colonial writers who believe that, as English no longer 'belongs' to a particular country, this allows the opportunity for diversity, for creative hybrids and innovative forms. Salman Rushdie, a writer who writes in English but is originally from an Indian cultural background, says that such writers, '. . . can't simply use the language the way the British did; that it needs remaking for our own purposes' (Rushdie, 1992, p. 17).

Whatever your background, keep in mind that there are many Englishnesses: you may be from Glasgow, Atlanta or Bangladesh and your characters may come from Jamaica, Morecambe or Hong Kong. The writing will be all the richer if you can access and integrate your own version of English as well as listening out for all those other voices.   *HL*

Further reading

Crystal, David, *The Cambridge Encyclopedia of the English Language* (Cambridge: Cambridge University Press, 2003).

Studies in World Literature in English and Postcolonialism, The Department of English Language and Literature, Fu Jen University, Taiwan at www.eng.fju.edu.tw/worldlit/world_link.htm (accessed 12 December 2006).

Thiong'o, Ngugi wa, *Decolonizing the Mind: The Politics of Language in African Literature* (Portsmouth, NH: Heinemann, 1981).

Rushdie, Salman, *Imaginary Homelands* (New York: Granta, 1992, p. 17).

envy

Even Shakespeare envied other writers their ability and success, as Bonnie Friedman points out in *Writing Past Dark*. 'Desiring this man's art, and that man's scope', he writes in his Sonnet 29. Most envy is not about the actual writing process or product, but about recognition, praise, success and money, which is putting the cart before the horse. Those things may come but only when the best work that you can do is completed. Envy misses the point because it undermines the very thing you need to produce good work: your own unique voice. As Friedman says,

> The antidote to envy is one's own work . . . Not the thinking about it. Not the assessing of it. But the doing of it. The answers you want can only come from the work itself. It drives the spooks away. (Friedman, 1994, p. 8)

HL

Further reading

Friedman, Bonnie, *Writing Past Dark* (New York: Harper Perennial, 1994).

epic

The epic, an ancient **poetic genre**, was originally a long narrative poem concerned with 'the tale of the tribe', that is the social or historical development of a people. Poets still turn to the epic today in order to explore big themes and ideas that move beyond the personal. This was particularly noticeable in the first half of the twentieth century when Ezra Pound wrote his *Cantos*, H.D. her *Helen in Egypt* and T. S. Eliot *The Wasteland*. Contemporary epics include Derek Walcott's *Omeros*, which explores the history of his own people of the Caribbean island of St Lucia. See also Frederick Turner's *The New World: An Epic*, a science fiction fantasy set in AD 2376. As with the **ballad**, the epic shows how it is still possible to use old genres and old stories to make new, relevant work.

HT

Further reading

H.D., *Helen in Egypt* (Manchester: Carcanet Press, 1985).

Eliot, T. S., *The Waste Land and Other Poems* (London: Penguin, 2003).

Pound, Ezra, *The Cantos* (London: Faber and Faber, 2003).

Turner, Frederick, *The New World: An Epic* (New Jersey: Princeton University Press, 1985).

Walcott, Derek, *Omeros* (London: Faber and Faber, 2002).

epistolary

An epistolary story or novel is written as a series of letters. Epistolary novels became popular in the eighteenth century – Samuel Richardson, for instance, wrote two novels in this form: *Pamela* and *Clarissa*. Jane Austen originally wrote *Pride and Prejudice* as an epistolary novel, but rewrote it in third person point of view. Epistolary novels are still written – Tim Parks' *Home Thoughts* and, most famously, Alice Walker's *The Color Purple.*

You don't have to write a story or novel that is entirely epistolary; using the form within a piece of fiction has a lot to recommend it. Letters are the fiction equivalent of soliloquies in drama; they allow for direct expression of thoughts and feelings by the character writing them. Whomever the letter is addressed to, it is in effect written to the reader, and the whole interior world of the character writing is opened up in an engaging way.

Using letters (or journal entries, which have a similar effect) is a way of making your text more various, more polyphonic. Anything that stops the novel being monolithic – whether it is the epistolary form or the use of multiple narrative – is desirable.   *RG*

experience

What you have done. Readers are fascinated with the question of whether or not your fiction is based on real experience. If the **protagonist** is a drug addict, the public may be surprised to learn that you never had a problem with drugs yourself. Some of what you write may be based on real experiences you have, but a lot of it won't. Fiction writers make up stuff – that's why it's called fiction.

Another aspect of the relationship between writing and experience is that writers in their twenties may not have a lot to say for themselves. (OK, Dickens wrote *Oliver Twist* when he was 25, but that's exceptional.) From this there is a suggestion that having something worth writing is linked to experience of the world. However, if this were absolutely true, older writers would always be better than younger ones.   *RG*

experimental poetry

Experimental poetry defines itself against traditional poetry derived from eighteenth- and nineteenth-century verse traditions. Many argue that all experimental poetry springs from early-twentieth-century modernism when a group of Anglo-American poets, known as the Imagists, defied poetic convention, particularly set forms and flowery 'poetic' language. Today, experimental poetry, aka linguistically innovative poetry (lip) or postmodern poetry, is diverse and eclectic in character. In the USA there is a strong and well-supported tradition of experimentation, although in the UK hardcore lip is still fighting its corner against die-hard convention.

In experimental poetry, there is often a more abstract use of language than in traditional poetry, and multiple meanings are likely to multiply even further. Text may be arranged on the page or screen in spatially unusual ways, as in open form and visual poetry. Richard Caddel's sequence, 'Ground', is a useful poem to explore in terms of open form: Caddel takes a simple sentence about 'throstles [thrushes] feeding' and rewrites and expands it into 11 poems, all with a very different structure on the page. This is also a prime example of **found poetry** using **repetition**.

At its simplest, visual poetry can consist of shape poems whose words delineate a picture of the object they describe, a form of poetry that children often enjoy. More subtle open form and visual poems can be highly abstract or experimental, such as the work of Edwin Morgan, a key figure in the Concrete poets, or Susan Howe, whose poems often involve criss-crossing lines of text.

It is worth exploring experimental poetry because it offers alternative ways of writing and thinking. Whether you become an innovator yourself or not, you can learn much about poetic craft and language by studying work which pushes poetry to its limits. The possibilities have become even wider over the last century, especially with the advent of the computer and the internet, where poets can create diverse structures and share them with each other in cyberspace.   *HT*

Writing ideas

- Take a poem that you or a friend have already written and try rearranging it on the page into three alternative versions, one focused on visual effect, one on sound and rhythm and one on form as embodiment of meaning.
- Try reading all four versions on the page and then aloud (allowing spaces to equate to pauses and note any differences in the effect). Is one of your

new ones better than the original or might the four make a sequence like Richard Caddel's?

Further reading

Caddel, Richard, *Quiet Music of Words* (Sheffield: West House Books, 2002).

Howe, Susan, *Singularities* (Middletown, CT: Wesleyan University Press, 1990).

Johnson, Nicholas, *FOIL: an exhibition anthology* (Buckfastleigh: Etruscan Books, 2000).

Levertov, Denise, *Selected Poems* (Northumberland: Bloodaxe Books, 1986).

Mengham, Rod and John Kinsella, *Vanishing Points* (Cambridge: Salt Publishing, 2004).

Morgan, Edwin, *Collected Poems* (Manchester: Carcanet, 1996).

O'Sullivan, Maggie, *Out of Everywhere: linguistically innovative poetry by women in North America and the UK* (London: Reality Street Editions, 1996).

Smith, Hazel, *The Writing Experiment: Strategies for Innovative Creative Writing* (Crows Nest, NSW: Allen and Unwin, 2005).

See also *WORDSTUFFS: the CITY and the BODY* by Hazel Smith, Roger Dean and Greg White (1998) at www.abc.net.au/arts/stuff-art/stuff-art99/stuff98/wordstuf/index.htm.

experimental writing

The history of writing is also the history of experimentation. The novel, when it first emerged in the seventeenth and eighteenth centuries, was considered such a *novelty* that the original description stuck. The short story, the film script, the television drama, were all, at one time, innovative writing forms. Wordsworth and Coleridge, long before they became safe pillars of the school curriculum, wrote, in 1798, that their new collection, *Lyrical Ballads*, should be 'considered as experiments . . . Readers . . . will perhaps frequently have to struggle with feelings of strangeness.'

The point is that experimentation continually arises in reaction to what may be considered tired and over-conventional forms. There are always some movers and shakers in each generation looking for ways to thumb their noses at the writing establishment. It may not help them to get onto the bestseller list, but for writers more interested in making it new than in making it rich and popular, there are a thousand and one ways of breaking the literary rules.

Many of the rules are currently being broken through the use of computer and communications technology, and many argue that the writing rule-book, possibly even the book itself, is soon to be made completely irrelevant by the internet with its new and proliferating creative forms. As these hypertextual and technological experiments are discussed elsewhere (see **IT**), this section will focus on literary experimentation within the book.

Many writers in the first half of the twentieth century, in reaction to nineteenth-century **realism** and influenced by psychoanalytical theories, were interested in the nature of the mind itself. James Joyce's *Ulysses* follows the thoughts, feelings, ideas and impressions of a number of characters traversing Dublin throughout a single day. The last chapter is made up of Molly Bloom's thoughts as she lies in bed, and so the text, like the wandering mind, is unpunctuated:

> Yes because he never did a thing like that before as ask to get his breakfast in bed with a couple of eggs since the *City Arms* hotel when he used to be pretending to be laid up with a sick voice doing his highness to make himself interesting . . .

This method of writing, usually called **stream of consciousness**, is a useful and playful technique, often used in writing classes to trigger ideas. However, consciousness in all its complexity is impossible to pin down to the page, although writers can have a lot of fun trying! The complexity is partly because the mind/world interface is constantly changing, but also because we are only able to write about the mind with the mind itself.

Reflexivity has intrigued many writers, triggering work which is sometimes called **metafiction**, where the writing refers to itself, drawing the reader's attention to its fictional status. Metafiction is often described as **postmodern** but there are examples as far back as Chaucer's *Canterbury Tales*. Many of us have been taught that self-consciousness, the intrusion of the author into the work, is a serious weakness, but for the writer interested in questioning the boundaries, such rules are a challenge rather than a restriction. Writers interested in having a go at metafiction could begin by writing a paragraph of a story then shifting into another voice which comments on the writing itself, on the writer's perspective and experience.

Another major area of experimentation is the love/hate relationship between the linear and non-linear. Georges Perec's *Life, A User's Manual* is a puzzle narrative, set in an apartment building with interconnected stories planned according to a grid design. The book can be read in a straightforward beginning-to-end way and also dipped into. *Hopscotch*, by Julio

Corteza, comes with its own table of instructions which help readers to find their way – to hop – through its numbered sections.

Jeff Noon, an experimental fiction writer himself, commented in a recent newspaper article (Noon, 2001) that film-makers and musicians are allowed much more freedom to experiment and play, using jumpcuts, freeze-frames and scratch methods, all of which could be interestingly applied to the narrative arts. One recent example of scratch, sample and jumpcut fiction is Mark Danielewski's *House of Leaves* (2000), a horror story based on a house which has a threatening labyrinth beneath it. This book is a series of layers and interconnections, a self-reflexive labyrinthine narrative in many voices, any one of which may be speaking truth, fiction or lies. There are blank pages, upside-down texts, footnotes and lists. *House of Leaves* is both linear and non-linear, sometimes in the form of a thesis, sometimes a film script, sometimes autobiography. One of the major influences on Danielewski, as on many contemporary writers and artists, is the work of the Argentinian writer Jorge Luis Borges, who died in 1989 and whose work explores the nature of time, space, fiction and non-fiction, leaving the reader never quite sure where one begins and the other ends.

This uncertainty, this rejection of clearly defined boundaries and forms, is perhaps the most challenging aspect of much contemporary experimental writing. At its worst it can seem deliberately obscure, exclusive and purpose-less. It is true that there has always been plenty of empty 'avant-garde' work: writing that aspires to be experimental for the sake of the experiment alone, which fails to make a real connection with readers. However, many writers, such as Danielewski, are making a serious attempt to describe the uncertain and half-formless world we live in using language that helps us to make sense out of these times and this place. Of course, we all need the reassuring and familiar pleasures of story and plot, answers and tied-up endings. But we also need looseness, openness, adventure and play and at times we may find it liberating to struggle, as Wordsworth said, with 'feelings of strangeness'.

HL

Writing ideas

1. New and experimentally creative work is, *by its nature*, unknown, unimagined. Your innovative ideas are likely to be very different from mine. Take risks. Make mistakes. Be brave. Make more mistakes. Be even braver.

2. List 20 ways to write a story. (*Backwards; only using words from music CD labels; out of all the things your mother said when you were a child . . .*) Pick the one that makes your heart beat faster.

Further reading

Borges, Jorge Luis, trans. A. Hurley, *Fictions* (London: Penguin, 2000).

Cortázar, Julio, trans. G. Rabassa, *Hopscotch* (London: The Harvill Press, 1998).

Danielewksi, Mark Z., *House of Leaves* (London: Transworld, 2000).

Joyce, James, *Ulysses* (London: Penguin, 2000).

Noon, Jeff, 'How to make a modern novel', *Guardian*, 10 January 2001.

Perec, Georges, trans. D. Bellos, *Life, A User's Manual* (London: David R. Godine, 1978).

Wordsworth, William and Samuel Taylor Coleridge, *Lyrical Ballads* (London: Penguin, 1999).

exposition

Background information that readers need if they are to make sense of a narrative. However, few pieces of advice about creating narrative are more memorable than Flannery O'Connor's on this score: 'Readers won't believe something just because you tell them it.' In other words, if the background information is very important, the writer will do well to show it to the reader. Raw, naked exposition – information on a plate – is peculiarly uninviting. *It had been a long day. Kirsty had been struggling with her filing system since lunchtime and too many people had called into her office and distracted her.* Want to read on?   RG

failure

Not realizing your ambitions. Failure is the writer's bedfellow. Most authors experience years of rejection before they get anywhere. Every writer I know has collected enough rejection letters from magazines and publishers to make a life-size origami Taj Mahal. Don't take it personally when it happens to you. It's something we all have to go through. When you receive rejection letters in the post, you may find it helps to bear in mind that it isn't you personally that is being turned down – it's your manuscript. The editors concerned have never met you, so why would they reject you? Remember, too, that acceptance is just a matter of your manuscript landing on the right person's desk on the right day. *RG*

feedback

What other people think of your work. Essential for writers. In 'The Rocky Road To Paper Heaven' (www.web.net/owtoad/road.html), Margaret Atwood's step-by-step account of how a work begins and eventually reaches the ideal reader, she lists the following as one of the stages: 'The work is shown to a few knowledgeable friends, if the writer is lucky enough to have some. Suggestions may be made, which the writer is free to accept or reject.' If a novelist of Atwood's stature needs feedback while a work is in production, you can bet you do, too. If you are studying at university, the feedback may come through a peer appraisal group or in a **workshop**. It may be that you have a writing buddy with whom you always trade work in progress. Wherever you find it, you won't be able to manage without feedback. *RG*

fiction

Made-up stories, usually in prose. From the Latin *fingere*, meaning 'to form or to create'. In theory, fiction involves a story and consists of material that has been imagined, although some fiction is partly or entirely based on real

64

experience. Usually when one talks of fiction it is prose fiction, but obviously a feature film is a work of fiction, too. Prose fiction comes in various lengths and forms: short stories, fairy tales, long stories, novellas, novels. For the most part, fiction is seen as something which engages the emotions as well as the mind of the reader. There are many fictional **genres** – romantic fiction, crime fiction and science fiction, for example. *RG*

fixed forms

Poetry written in fixed forms adheres to one or more of the following: a set **metre**, number of syllables per line, rhyme scheme, number of lines and number of stanzas. Key examples are the **sonnet**, **villanelle** and **haiku**. Ideally, at first reading, it is the sound, language and meaning that should compel the reader's attention: they should not be calculating syllables, lines and rhyme schemes in order to crack the code. Most commonly this is achieved by crafty **lineation**. In 'Terza Rima SW19', Carol Ann Duffy's title cheekily draws attention to her use of a three-line stanza form in which the second line of each tercet rhymes with the first and third line of the next stanza. Despite this, she succeeds in creating a flow of language *across* the formal barriers of line and stanza ends, thus diverting our attention from the fixed form onto the love affair evoked. For those who enjoy the complex word calculations posed by fixed forms, it is a joy to discover or invent a new one. Others regard them as outdated curiosities and never touch one in their whole poetic careers. *HT*

Further reading

Duffy, Carol Ann, *Standing Female Nude* (London: Anvil Press Poetry, 1985).

Fry, Stephen, *The Ode Less Travelled: Unlocking the Poet Within* (London: Hutchinson Books, 2005).

flailing and kvetching

Anne Lamott's resonant term, from *Bird By Bird – Some Instructions on Writing and Life*, for what the novelist goes through to find a satisfactory plot. 'Kvetch' is Yiddish and means 'to complain habitually'. Imagine a writer throwing himself (or inanimate objects) about the room and complaining ceaselessly and you have a fair picture of the agonies we go through trying to arrive at a plot that seems right. If you aren't prepared to put up with flailing and *kvetching*, think about trying some other line of work. *RG*

Further reading

Lamott, Anne, *Bird By Bird – Some Instructions on Writing and Life* (New York: Anchor Books, 1995).

flashback

A scene in a story or novel that occurred prior to the now of the narrative. Use sparingly. If you are going to ask readers to leave your narrative, which you have constructed with enormous care to be as engaging as possible, you had better have a very good reason for it. Why? Because once your flashback is over, you will have to build your narrative again from scratch. If you still want to use a flashback, do bear in mind that readers will need signposts in and out of it. If you don't place markers at the start and end of a flashback, the reader has every right to believe that the story is continuing chronologically, which will be confusing. Markers can be as simple as your **protagonist** looking at the clock at each end of the flashback.   RG

fonts

Letter designs. My version of Word has 146 fonts, most of which are legible and in English. It is extremely unlikely that an editor, whether at a literary magazine or at a publishing house, is interested in seeing more than two or three of them. I've been told that one should always submit in Courier New, but the truth is that this is only necessary when submitting screenplays. For everything else, Times New Roman and Arial are probably what editors most welcome. Helvetica isn't going to alienate anyone, but if you submit a manuscript in Little Brat or Curlz MT, you are effectively saying, 'Please bin'.   RG

found poetry

Many poems incorporate writing not composed by the author of the poem, but 'found' elsewhere. Found text can originate from literary as well as factual books, websites, advertisements, road signs, graffiti, official letters, even words overheard. The found text may be placed by the poet in a montage with other found words or original writing.

When using found text, you need to decide whether to acknowledge your sources. Plagiarism is not regarded as a major issue in poetry, but it is not acceptable to pass off another poet's work as your own. Quotation marks or italics may be enough to signify that text originates elsewhere, but for substantial usage, a footnote is needed.

Lorine Niedecker's work, which explores significant lives, provides a fine example of the use of found text – she incorporates (often tiny) phrases from her subjects' writing in order to build a picture of their lives. Her titles, such as 'Darwin' and 'Thomas Jefferson Inside', show the origins of the quoted text, thus avoiding the need for references. The selection and arrangement of found text gives the words new and striking resonance.   *HT*

Writing ideas
- Read a non-fiction book that interests you (a biography, a book of natural history, an IT manual).
- Select tiny fragments of language that appeal to you for their language, sound or significance.
- Using only ten words of your own, keep paring down and rearranging your found words to make a poem.

Further reading
Niedecker, Lorine, *Collected Works* (Berkeley: University of California Press, 2002).

garrets

Artists in their garrets: an appealingly romantic notion. However, you have to eat. In the arts, there will always be individuals with trust funds or rich spouses. They're the lucky ones. The rest of us need a day-job while we're shaping our masterpiece, even if it's only part-time. This is not to say that writers don't need to go out on a limb, or be single-minded, but a touch of pragmatism is useful. Besides, writers need some **experience** of the world in order to write anything that the world will find credible.   *RG*

gender

Let's get one thing straight (or not, as the case may be): gender and sex are not the same thing. Sex is a biological fact, determined at the moment of conception. Those of us with two X chromosomes will be female; those with an X and a Y chromosome will be male. Gender is the way that society constructs female and male identities. So a person born biologically female is expected to behave in a feminine way, and a person born biologically male is expected to behave in a masculine way. While sex may be a biological constant (for most), gender is not. As societies change, so do their expectations of gender roles. In Renaissance England, for example, a woman who published a book in her own name was outrageously transgressive, and brought shame upon her family. Making the contents of her mind public was akin to sexual incontinence. Elizabeth Cary was the first woman in England, so far as we know, to write and publish a play in her own name. When *The Tragedy of Mariam* was published in 1613, King James thought her authorship a joke because it was too good for a woman to have written and her mortified husband cut her off without a penny.

Times have changed, but perhaps not as much as we like to think. We may resist the stereotypes that dress little girls in pink frills and little boys in superhero outfits, but individuals who don't conform to gender expectations are often subject to social pressure. A strong, assertive woman may be seen as pushy and aggressive, while an emotionally expressive man may be seen as weak.

What does this mean for practising writers? There are two main considerations: how you are treated as an author because of your gender; and how your gender may influence what you write. Are male and female writers treated differently by publishers and readers?

There is still a general perception that women writers are at a disadvantage, especially those who want to be taken 'seriously'. Indeed, Debbie Taylor of *Mslexia* magazine defines the word 'mslexia' as 'a difficulty, more prevalent in women, with getting published'. Taylor goes on to list some damning statistics: in the twentieth century, 96 per cent of Nobel Prize for Literature winners were men; from 1969 to 1998, 69 per cent of Booker Prize winners were men; from 1971 to 1997, 90 per cent of Whitbread Poetry Prize winners were men; and perhaps most surprisingly, given the stereotypes discussed above, 62 per cent of Betty Trask Award for Romantic Fiction winners (1984 to 1995) were men.

On the other hand, male writers may be forgiven for thinking they're getting a rough deal. Women have got the Orange Prize for fiction and magazines such as *Mslexia* (written by women for women) setting up women-only poetry and short-story competitions. I don't know of any equivalent men-only prizes or publications, and I'll bet that there would be an outcry should one be attempted. So, is it right that women should enjoy positive discrimination as a way of compensating for the disadvantages they've suffered? Or is such special treatment an implicit acknowledgement of their inferiority? It's a debate that looks set to run and run.

Your gender may affect how, where and if you get published, but does it actually influence your writing? Almost certainly it does, but can consciousness of this influence be used to positive effect? Virginia Woolf was keenly alert to the effects of gender on a person's writing. In her classic essay *A Room of One's Own* Woolf imagines Shakespeare's sister, a woman with the same talent as Shakespeare, and concludes that she would have ended up buried under a crossroads, thwarted by her society. Indeed, this work has been seen as a manifesto for women writers in their struggle to claim the time and space they need in order to work.

And yet Woolf has something more subtle to say about gender and its implications:

> . . . it is fatal for anyone who writes to think of their sex. It is fatal to be a man or woman pure and simple; one must be woman-manly or man-womanly. (Woolf, 2004, p. 120)

Woolf puts her idea into practice with the fantastical biography *Orlando*, where the eponymous hero begins life as a swashbuckling Elizabethan nobleman until he wakes up one day and discovers that he has become a she. Lady Orlando travels through the centuries until she ends up as a woman writer in Woolf's own time. This gives Woolf plenty of scope for a satirical look at gender relations, but beneath all the good clean cross-dressing fun, Woolf is making a valuable point about gender and writing:

> Different though the sexes are, they intermix. In every human being a vacillation from one sex to another takes place, and often it is only the clothes that keep the male or female likeness, while underneath the sex is the very opposite of what is above. (Woolf, 2000, pp. 132–3)

Therefore, if writing is to be a convincing evocation of the human state, it must be neither masculine nor feminine, but inclusive of both elements, open to all facets of human experience. One way of making a conscious effort to do this is to write as the gender you aren't. Successful novelist Rose Tremain states that 'I believe I put something of myself into all the characters in my novels, male as well as female' (www.book-club.co.nz/features/rosetremain.htm). This is impressively demonstrated in her first novel, *Sadler's Birthday*, which is told from the point of view of an elderly man. Similarly, Robert Graves in *Wife to Mr Milton* provides a fine example of a male author writing in the first person female, and a seventeenth-century one at that. *UH*

Writing ideas

1. *Writing as the gender you aren't*

   If you usually experience the world from a feminine perspective, try writing from a masculine perspective, or vice versa. Make it more interesting by choosing a character older or younger than yourself, or remote from you in space and/or time. Mix it up further by trying to write from the point of view of somebody who has changed, or is in the process of changing, gender. See what happens.

2. *Try a nom-de-plume*

   Do a 'George Eliot' and give yourself a pen name which changes your gender. Or try a name which gives away no gender at all (J. K. Rowling, A. S. Byatt). Monitor how this affects responses to your work. Do you write differently when using this name? How do readers respond to your pen name? Do you receive more or fewer rejections?

Further reading

Book-Club, 'Conversation with Rose Tremain' (available online at www.book-club. co.nz/features/rosetremain.htm (accessed 12 December 2006).

Cary, Elizabeth, *The Tragedy of Mariam, Fair Queen of Jewry*, eds Barry Ferguson and Margaret Weller (Berkeley: University of California Press, 1994).

Graves, Robert, *Wife to Mr Milton* (London: Penguin, 1968).

Mslexia – for women who write, www.mslexia.co.uk (accessed 12 December 2006).

Orange Prize for Fiction, www.orangeprize.co.uk (accessed 12 December 2006).

Taylor, Debbie, 'Three Cures for *Mslexia*', www.mslexia.co.uk/menu/curesformslexia1. html (accessed 12 December 2006).

Tremain, Rose, *Sadler's Birthday* (London: Vintage Paperback, 1999; first published 1976).

Woolf, Virginia, *A Room Of One's Own* (London: Penguin Great Ideas, 2004; first published 1928).

——, *Orlando* (London: Penguin Classics, 2000; first published 1928).

genius

A unique creative talent – Shakespeare, Mozart. For most of us, that level of creativity is out of reach. However, Jane Hopkins defined genius as 'an infinite capacity for taking pains', which is something to which we can all aspire. Equally helpful is the original Creative Writing expert, Dorothea Brande, who, in *Becoming a Writer*, argues that the work of art 'takes shape and has its origin outside the region of the conscious intellect' (Brande, 1996, p. 149). She contends that we all have our genius, which lies in the unconscious mind and which we can learn to tap.   *RG*

genre

A category of, for instance, novel or film. Examples in the former include crime fiction and science fiction, and, in the latter, film noir and romantic comedy. Each genre has its own set of conventions and, probably for this reason alone, genre fiction is regarded as somehow inferior or less creative than work that falls outside of any genre. There's a definite sense that if you're producing genre work, you are writing with an eye to the market. However, there is an argument that all fiction is genre fiction and that literary fiction is just one more genre.   *RG*

gestation

Development period or process. Picture the hen sitting on the egg, the bun cooking in the oven. Gestation takes time and these images suggest the way that things develop gradually. An idea gestates in the way a snowball grows as it rolls down hill, or in the way magnets attract iron filings to themselves. Given time, the dough becomes the loaf, the tadpole becomes the frog. Less metaphorically, gestation is a matter of you leaving an idea to soak in your **unconscious** mind and seeing what messages it sends back. If you think you can produce a short story in one sitting, you are leaving out a vital element of the process: gestation time. *RG*

grammar

The system of rules by which words are put together to form sentences. **Syntax** – the order that words come in a sentence – is part of grammar, as is **punctuation**. If you are unwittingly ungrammatical, you will lose all credibility for readers. Your characters may be ungrammatical. That's fine. But if you write about 'hating them formal occasions', it doesn't really matter how strong your story is, how sympathetic your narrator; readers will assume you can't know what you're talking about. Of course, stream of consciousness breaks some of the rules of grammar, but it's clear that people who have used it – Joyce and Woolf, for instance – understood grammar. *RG*

graphic novel

A graphic novel is a book-length comic. That word *comic* is misleading, implying a work that, even if it's not funny, is likely to be simplistic and formulaic. These days comics still have enough sticky-footed men and bug-eyed monsters to satisfy the child in all of us, but there are also many grown-up alternatives.

Some fine examples include the harrowing *Maus* by Art Spiegelman, which tells the story of the Jews in Poland under the Nazis, with Jews depicted as mice and the Nazis as cats. *Maus* also includes a graphic personal account of the process of writing the book. *Watchmen*, by Alan Moore, is a crime thriller with a dark tone and depth of character, which also makes social and political comment.

Many graphic novel writers work as part of a team, preparing a storyboard and graphic style collectively. However, if you want to produce the whole thing yourself, you will need illustrative as well as writing skills *HL*

Further reading

Eisner, Will, *Comics and Sequential Art* (Cincinatti, OH: North Light Books, 2001).
Moore, Alan, *Watchmen* (London: Titan Books, 2006).
Spiegelman, Art, *The Complete Maus* (London: Penguin, 2003).

haiku

The Japanese-derived haiku is the most popular of the syllabic **fixed forms** of poetry. These are poems based on the number of syllables in a line; a haiku has three lines of five, seven and five syllables respectively. Traditionally the haiku used natural symbolism to provoke meditation on a wider theme, but contemporary haiku writers have expanded subject matter, symbolism and, in some cases, the number of syllables used. See also the englyn, the cinquain and the ghazal for even more complex and playful forms.　　*HT*

Further reading

Watts, Maureen, 'Working with Traditional Forms' in John Timpane and Maureen Watts, *Poetry for Dummies* (New York: For Dummies, 2001).
Modern Haiku at www.modernhaiku.org.

hero

From Beowulf to Batman, great stories have always needed heroes: someone larger than life, willing to risk it all in the cause of truth and justice. The kind of person we'd like to be. However, if we want to craft a memorable hero, not a comic-book figure but an individual, we need to understand the psychological processes at work. As Christopher Booker states:

> He has to show that he is acting selflessly, in some cause outside himself. He has to show himself inwardly strong, determined, totally self-reliant. In the end, as the final key in the lock, he has to have superior understanding, a clear vision of what he has to do. (Booker, 2004, p. 246)

A hero has to suffer and grow spiritually before he can succeed. But no one likes a goody-two-shoes. Almost every hero you can think of has some kind of weakness, the archetypal Achilles heel. Superman dreads kryptonite, Indiana Jones is terrified of snakes, Luke Skywalker has an unspeakably evil father. And at some point in their journeys all these heroes have to confront and overcome their weaknesses. It's this flaw that makes their heroic qualities shine all the more brightly. *UH*

Further reading

Booker, Christopher, *The Seven Basic Plots: Why We Tell Stories* (London: Continuum, 2004).

heroine

This word carries with it a weight of expectation:

> The heroine is the one who carries the spears but does not hurl them. The one who dresses well but does not dirty her nails in the fight. The one who lies down in a glass casket, until revived by an awakening kiss. (Yolen, 1998, p. xviii)

Reading between the lines, a traditional heroine makes herself useful, looks good at all times, and refrains from being proactive in any way. The concept of the heroine seems to call for something other than straight-forward heroics. And yet despite all those Snow Whites waiting to be rescued by handsome princes, there have always been sisters who do it for themselves. Shakespeare's Cleopatra seduced some of the most powerful men in the world, ruled a great country, and played shamelessly on her sexuality in order to get what she wanted. Defoe's Moll Flanders was

> Twelve Year a Whore, five times a Wife (Whereof once to her own Brother), Twelve Year a Thief, Eight Year a Transported Felon in Virginia, at last grew Rich, liv'd Honest, and died a Penitent. (Defoe, 1998, p. 1)

Gender and sexuality seem to be major components of memorable heroines: rare creatures who can retain their femininity while being heroic. Think of Princess Leia in *Star Wars* shooting stormtroopers without disturbing a hair on her immaculately coiffed head, or dressed in a very skimpy bikini while throttling Jabba the Hutt with the chain he has used to imprison her. Lara Croft in *Tomb Raider*, Buffy the Vampire Slayer, Charlie's Angels . . . they can do everything a hero does *and* look good in heels. *UH*

Further reading

Defoe, Daniel, *Moll Flanders* (Oxford: Oxford Paperbacks, 1998; first published 1722).

Shakespeare, William, *Antony and Cleopatra* (London: Arden Shakespeare, 1995; written around 1606).

Yolen, Jane, 'Foreword', *Fearless Girls, Wise Women & Beloved Sisters: Heroines in Folktales from Around the World*, ed. Kathleen Ragan (London: W.W. Norton & Company, 1998).

hooks

Often, though not always, a reader-question. (Readers may also be hooked by an author's voice, a character or a setting.) If your fiction is without reader-questions it will very quickly be without readers. My favourite hook is the opening line of Russell Hoban's story 'Telling Stories': 'I wonder if this happens to a lot of men?' The reader-question, the hook, is this: what is 'it'? In a short story, the hook should arrive on the first page and ideally as early on the first page as possible. In a novel, the hook should appear within the first few pages, certainly within the first chapter. One hook will not be enough to sustain your readers through a story; more need to appear as the narrative progresses.   *RG*

house style

A publisher's rules about presentation of manuscripts. Once you have your publication deal, a contract will arrive and it will usually make some stipulations about the presentation of your manuscript, or about the way they are going to present the book when it goes into print. In the world of fiction, this may not be a matter of many stipulations; they might only ask that text is to be double-spaced. In the world of **non-fiction** – for example, in a book like this – the contract will specify quite a lot: whether single or double speech marks are to be used; that all dashes are to be double dashes; etc.   *RG*

imagery

Figurative language. Poetic images work by comparison, likening one thing to another. The most widely known forms of imagery are the **metaphor** and the **simile**, learned by every schoolchild from time immemorial. In the simile, attention is drawn to the figurative comparison by use of the word 'like' or 'as'; in the metaphor, it is not. Both can have the effect of bringing a subject closer to us, by comparing it to something familiar, and/or of distancing it, by making us look at it in a new way. Craig Raine's poem 'A Martian Sends a Postcard Home' is a series of metaphors, such as 'Rain is when the earth is television', designed to defamiliarize the world as we know it. Raine founded the movement Martianism, which specialized in striking metaphor.

As the phrase 'dead metaphor' suggests, images can quickly become outdated. After centuries of English and American poetry, it becomes harder to be original in the use of imagery. Poets these days adopt a variety of responses to the problem of metaphor. They might use it more subtly or sparingly than in the past or, conversely, draw attention to its use in a self-conscious or postmodern manner. Bob Cobbing, in his poem 'a good fuck makes me feel like custard', extends this already provocative simile to the point of absurdity with eight variations on the image. This makes his simile also a conceit, an elaborately extended metaphor or simile taking up a sub-stantial proportion of a poem. There are a plethora of specialized terms for specific types of imagery, such as personification (referring to animals or objects as if they were human) and animism (referring to humans as if they were animals). Metonymy focuses on the connection between things that are naturally close to each other; for example, when the part is substituted for the whole, as in crown for queen.

The symbol is a less limited image which often refers to a more abstract idea; some symbols are conventional, such as the rose for love or the dove for peace, but usually, the poet does not explicitly state what his symbol represents, allowing creative guessing games for the reader.

However, many poets would still argue that 'poetry is metaphor' (Wallace Stevens) and certainly metaphoric language is at the heart of poetic thinking and even language itself (all words make reference to something outside of themselves).   *HT*

Further reading

Cobbing, Bob, *Kob Bok* (Buckfastleigh: Etruscan Books, 1999).
Raine, Craig, *A Martian Sends a Postcard Home* (Oxford: Oxford University Press, 1979).

immediacy

The sense of being right there in the story. Immediacy is a concept at the centre of mainstream, realist fiction writing. When a novel or short story is immediate, it is because an author has created an illusion of reality, a theatre or cinema in the mind of the reader where a kind of virtual reality takes place. The words on the page make something appear to happen tangibly, right here, right now. Immediacy gives readers the impression that they are *there* in the fictional world, experiencing what the point-of-view character is experiencing at the very moment he or she is having the experience.

Writing immediate fiction has to do with the difference between *telling* and *showing*. The former is not immediate, whereas the latter is. You may well find it hard to discern whether or not your fiction is immediate. With practice, though, it can become second nature. A good starting place is with the author: if an author is apparent in a particular passage, is in evidence alongside the characters, the fiction will more than likely not be consistently immediate. This authorial presence may well result in **omniscient narration**.

Imagine an eighteenth- or nineteenth-century author, probably with a long beard or in a long dress (though most likely not both at the same time), comfortable in a leather-bound, winged armchair, explaining the background to the story, or outlining the protagonist's characteristics – he or she, in this narrative mode, will not be creating a sense of immediacy for the reader. Here's one well-known nineteenth-century author, Charles Dickens, at the beginning of *Bleak House*, holding forth in omniscient mode from an armchair that has been plumped down right smack in the middle of the playing area:

> Never can there come fog too thick, never can there come mud and mire too deep, to assort with the groping and floundering condition which this High Court of Chancery, most pestilent of hoary sinners, holds this day, in the sight of heaven and earth.

On such an afternoon, if ever, the Lord High Chancellor ought to be sitting here – as here he is – with a foggy glory round his head, softly fenced in with crimson cloth and curtains . . . On such an afternoon, some score of members of the High Court of Chancery bar ought to be – as they are here – mistily engaged in one of the ten thousand stages of an endless cause, tripping one another up on slippery precedents . . . and making a pretence of equity with serious faces, as players might.
(Dickens, 1853, p. 2)

Where is the omniscient narrator in this passage? In all the generalizations ('On such an afternoon . . .'), explanations ('Never can there come . . .' and 'ought to be . . .') and asides to the reader (' – as they are here – '). Why is Dickens not creating a sense of immediacy for the reader? Simply because the author, or omniscient narrator, has become an intermediary between character and reader (or between action and reader). He gets in the way; he prevents instant access to the story.

Focusing on the problem with that notion of an intermediary, or a middleman, is perhaps a useful way to understand how a sense of immediacy may be created for the reader. It has to do with proximity. In a narrative, whether it's a novel or a memoir – the fictional nature of the writing isn't relevant here – readers will experience the **plot**, the **action**, through the filter of the viewpoint character's consciousness (see **point of view**) if you close the distance between all three, between reader, viewpoint character and action. If readers feel *as one* with the **protagonist**, and the protagonist is right in the midst of the action (rather than telling you about it, or looking back on it from some distance away), you will have created an immediate, vicarious experience for them. In Richard Ford's rites of passage novel *Wildlife*, the narrator's father sets fire to the home of his wife's lover. In the aftermath of the fire, Joe, the narrator, approaches his dad:

I took off my jacket when I got to my father, and I put it over his boot where it was burning, and I held it down hard and put my arms around it to close the flames.
'I can't really see myself now,' my father said . . . His face was very pale, and both his hands looked black as though they'd been burned . . . 'Your mother's not there,' he said to me very calmly. 'Don't worry. I established that.' Light snow was beginning to collect on both of us.
'Why did you light this?' I said, holding on to his foot.

'To get things back on track, I guess,' he said, looking down at his hands in his lap. (Ford, 1990, pp. 149–50)

In this passage, we are in Joe's viewpoint, his perspective. We see what he sees, hear what he hears; we inhabit his situation directly. As a result, we vicariously experience it – the burned, disturbed father, the perplexing act of arson he has committed – and we both deduce and experience Joe's emotional response. (Shock? Dismay?) All we have is what happens, perceived from right within the character, right within the situation. No sign of Richard Ford at all, because Ford has immersed himself in his character, Joe, and the situation.

The dramatic conflict in a work of fiction plays a significant part in offering the reader an immediate experience. If immediacy is a matter of immersing readers in the character and the story, a matter of compelling them to read on, it will obviously be helpful if there is something at stake, if your fiction is built on a **conflict** of some kind, a dramatic situation. **Dramatization** and immediacy are the Tweedledee and Tweedledum of a compelling narrative. Immediacy puts you right there in the viewpoint character's shoes and dramatization raises the questions that keep you turning the pages. (Will she get her man? Will the innocent man be exonerated? Will the fugitive escape?)

Crucial, too, is your **style**, the words you use and the way you arrange them in sentences. Here clarity, concision and **directness** play an important role. Anton Chekhov, the nineteenth-century writer who has so profoundly influenced twentieth- and twenty-first-century short-story writing, famously called for clear, economical expression, arguing that 'good writing should be grasped at once, in a second'. *RG*

Writing ideas

1. *Less is more*

   Look at the clutter in the Dickens extract compared to the relative cleanness of the Ford. Write a scene in which a man and woman who know each other very well meet for coffee in Starbucks. They have been friends for almost three years, and now one of them wants their involvement to deepen. Follow Chekhov's advice and write as clearly and succinctly as you can.

2. *Writing with the senses*

   One way of heightening the reality of a piece of writing is to allow the reader's senses to become engaged. We live in a terribly visual world – note the dominance of screens of one kind or another and images in twenty-first-century culture – and most of us tend to write as if we only have one sense: sight. Take the couple in the last exercise out onto the street, and bring your other senses into play. Is it raining? How will that feel on the skin of your viewpoint character? Is this a busy city street? What will your characters be able to hear? To smell? Suppose they kiss (however chastely) when they part; that will involve both smell and taste.

Further reading

Atkinson, Kate, *Behind The Scenes At The Museum* (London: Black Swan, 1996).
Ford, Richard, *Wildlife* (London: Flamingo, 1991).
Mitchell, David, *Cloud Atlas* (London: Sceptre, 2005).
Tyler, Anne, *The Amateur Marriage* (London: Vintage, 2005).

in medias res

The idea of beginning a story in the middle of the action. The Roman lyric poet Horace came up with the notion and coined the phrase *in medias res*, which literally means 'in the middle of things'. Nothing has changed. Your story begins with the blue touchpaper on the firework burning, not with the trip down to the firework shop.   *RG*

inciting incident

The event that sets a plot in motion. In *Great Expectations*, it is when the convict Magwitch asks young Pip to get him food and a file. In *The Catcher in the Rye*, it is when Holden Caulfield is expelled from his prep school. Although often dramatic, the inciting incident doesn't have to be; Henry James said it can be as little as a woman putting her hand on the table and looking at you in 'that certain way'.   *RG*

index cards

A planning technique. The idea is that you use index cards, briefly summarizing each scene on a separate card. The main advantage of this over doing the same consecutively on screen is that it allows you the possibility of reorganizing your plot: once the cards are laid out on the carpet or the kitchen table, it's easy to adjust the order of things. Somehow the physicality of this is always more efficient than using 'cut and paste' to attempt the same in a computer file.   *RG*

influences

Authors or works that inform you and your work. I once interviewed a pop star who dismissed the idea that he might have any influences. When I persisted, arguing that everyone is influenced by somebody, he hung up. Everyone is always influenced by someone. The kind of writing you end up producing will undoubtedly synthesize elements of the approaches of the different authors you love. At some point, you will be conscious of emulating the techniques or styles of your favourite writers, but sometimes you won't even be aware of doing it. To make sure your own writing is as strong and rich as it can be, you should be reading as widely and ambitiously as you can – because what you consume and what you produce are closely linked.   *RG*

intentions

What you had in mind in creating a piece of work. To you, your intentions in crafting a piece of work are infinitely interesting and useful, but to your reader they scarcely matter. Once your work enters the public domain, it belongs to readers and they are allowed to make of it what they will. It matters not one whit that you thought you were writing a work of fiction that shows a man's sensitive appreciation of women; if your readers find it sexist nonsense, that's their prerogative. Where intentions are of use to you is in your reflections about your work. For instance, it may be instructive to look at the differences between intention and outcome.   *RG*

IT

The writer's world has been transformed by computers since the 1980s. Back then, most writers still worked at a typewriter, laboriously editing and proof-reading by hand, then retyping the next draft. 'Cut and paste' meant just that: scissors and Pritt stick. Now whole chapters can be re-ordered in a few clicks; the **spellcheck** replaces the dictionary; software systems lay out the page to publishing standard. For today's children in the wealthier nations, computers have always been part of their educational furniture: for the rest of us, it's catch up or die. Mostly this is a good thing – it certainly beats wrestling with inky typewriter ribbons – but even if we have our doubts, there isn't the slightest likelihood that a few pen-wielding luddites can stop the computer train in its digital tracks.

In this period of rapid evolutionary innovation, any attempt to predict which new electronic forms will become part of the artistic and popular mainstream is likely to be seriously flawed. When the printing press was first invented, surely no one could have imagined the widespread popularity of narrative fiction, let alone *War and Peace* or *The Da Vinci Code*. All that is possible is to point to some of the fresh creative opportunities that this technology offers to the writer. Word processors may have streamlined the mechanics of writing but, more significantly, just as the printing press and the codex book revolutionized the literary world, so the key features of computers and communications technologies are altering the way we interact with language and texts. Innovative forms and genres, new kinds of writer, new ways of reading and publishing are emerging all the time. Magan Sapnar and Ingrid Ankerson comment that this is a crucial creative field, 'One which challenges . . . writers and artists, to discover extraordinary ways to make sense of language, art, and narrative' (Sapnar and Ankerson, 2004).

Millions of people are now playing online games and it is instructive that most of these games have underlying dramatic narratives. There are characters, often schematic and crudely drawn. There are plots, mainly predictable and repetitive with little in the way of complexity or nuance. But these are early days: it took film many years before its full potential began to be realized. Two key features of these online games are interactivity and collaboration. Players become active participants; they can influence the action to some extent: they make choices. In this way the traditional relationship between writer and reader, director and audience is changing; boundaries are blurring and collaborative play enables players to take on characters and to interact with each other in the fictional space created for them by the games producers.

There is clearly a need here for writers who are interested in developing characters, stories and plots that are *not* simplistic, crude and schematic. But just as writers for film had to learn how to imagine their stories through image and camera shot as well as though word and description, so writers for this online medium will need to learn to use the qualities these early games rely on: interactivity; multiple pathways; multi-player collaboration.

Some writers are attempting to develop online work that crosses over from conventional fiction. Geoff Ryman's work *253 – A Novel for the Internet* is a story built around the passengers making a single, fateful journey on a London underground train. Instead of chapters, the sections are based on the train coaches. You can read each person's story in any order you choose, but there is also a dramatic underlying narrative, plenty of small stories and witty, intelligent digressions. There are no pictures or multimedia, just text organized to work online interactively.

The *Myst* and *Riven* series, produced by Ubisoft, are another interesting example, a huge multi-world fantasy saga which intersperses text, game play, storyline and characters, all without guns, racing cars or gore. Although this is an ambitious attempt at interactive and complex immersivity, it lacks character development and so feels more like an elaborate puzzle than a story. However, this series is a must-see for writers interested in the creative potential of IT, if only to learn why it doesn't quite work at the level of narrative.

The internet is often irritating and overwhelming and you need to discriminate between the useful and the dross, but, apart from the scale, this confusion is similar to many people's first experience of a library. There are also major accessibility issues, but technology is racing ahead and it can't be long before we will be able to download all books onto some kind of handheld device with a screen, just as it's now possible to download some audio texts onto MP3 players. Even if you intend to stick to conventional forms, online research, online publishing, **blogs,** e-zines, chatrooms and support groups are proliferating and many are useful for writers.

There are doomsayers who view the internet as a threat to literary culture, but there's no real evidence of the book disappearing just yet. Most big bookshops are overflowing with new titles and enthusiastic readers; book groups are springing up all over the place and there are far more writers than there were 50 years ago. In fact, the internet is encouraging whole new generations to engage with the written word in ways that could not have been imagined a short time ago. It is much more likely that digital forms will develop alongside conventional print just as film and stage drama co-exist beside television and books. If you're not technophobic, then at least *look* at some of the wonders and the dross out there. You may even get hooked into having a go at interactive writing or multimedia play for yourself.   *HL*

Writing ideas

Any writer with reasonable computer competence could produce an interactive fiction, using Ryman's *253* as a model. Use a web-authoring tool (Frontpage, within Microsoft Office, for example) to tell a story using three characters. Let the reader choose the order of reading. Create diversions, as Ryman does, but make sure the story has a dramatic narrative.

Further reading
Dorner, Jane, *The Internet: A Writer's Guide* (London: A&C Black, 2000).

IT

Garrand, Timothy, *Writing for Multimedia* (Burlington, MA: Butterworth Heinemann, 2001).

Ryman, Geoff, *253 – A Novel for the Internet* (www.ryman-novel.com, accessed 13 December 2006). (Also a book: London: Flamingo, 1998).

Sapnar, Magan, and Ingrid Ankerson, www.poemsthatgo.com (Winter Issue 2004: 15, accessed 13 December 2006).

journals

In one sense, a journal, like a diary, is a private place where one may pour out thoughts and feelings. A writer's journal may well have this function, but it has many others besides. It's a place where you can give birth to your writing and nurture it, a place where you may assemble and develop the resources that will become your novel or screenplay or poem. Keeping a journal is a way of ensuring that your ideas won't get lost; one of the few certainties in a writer's life is that ideas that don't get written down will disappear. In recording not only your ideas, but also what you see and think and feel, you will find that you are able to capture the freshness of these things – like freezing food. In this extract from his notebooks, the nineteenth-century American novelist Nathaniel Hawthorne records finding a young woman who has drowned:

> Her arms had stiffened in the act of struggling; and were bent before her, with the hands clenched. She was the very image of a death-agony; and when the men tried to compose her figure, her arms would still return to the same position; indeed it was almost impossible to force them out of it for an instant. (Hawthorne, in Oates (ed.), p. 247)

For the value of recording reality in just such a way, Paul Magrs recommends

> think[ing] of your notebooks as a way of capturing the things that go through your head. Think of them as yourself, your memory and everything you witness; all of it distilled. In notebooks and journals we see writers in mid-flight. (Magrs, in Bell and Magrs (eds), 2001, p. 10)

The journal is also a place for you to work out. In *Wild Mind*, Natalie Goldberg talks about *writing practice*. Like piano practice, it is something we ought to be doing on a daily basis. Why? Because it will get you into the habit of thinking in words, of putting things into writing so that your use of language becomes more fluent and eloquent. According to Anaïs Nin, writing

> as one practises the piano every day keeps one nimble, and then when the great moments of inspiration come, one is in good form, supple and smooth. (Newman et al., 2004, p. 10)

More particular uses of the journal are many and various. Here's an indicative list that may expand your thinking about what your journal may contain. Notes – on what you read, on films you watch; research of ideas and information you undertake for your writing; recording of overheard dialogue; description of what you see and hear whilst *in situ* on a beach or in a café; recording of your day-to-day experience – for instance, on holiday; post-its, clippings and photographs; first drafts of poems or stories (because you aren't always at the screen when you need to write); reflection about work in progress, about you as a writer – or as a reader; words you would like to use.

So much for why and how you may use a writer's journal. Now let's look at the form it may take. First of all, it's important to understand that **notebooks** and journals are part and parcel of the same thing and each will serve a similar purpose. The one way in which we should differentiate between the two forms is that a notebook will usually be portable and a journal will usually not be. I hesitate to lay down the law and recommend that writers should always have a notebook about their person. I would say, though, that it will make your life easier if you do (see **notebooks**).

Next, be aware that a journal may take a variety of forms. The most obvious variation is the one I've just mentioned: that between the notebook which will slip into your pocket and something larger that won't. Some of your journal writing may take place in blank-paged or lined books commercially produced for just that purpose, but much of it may be in files on your computer. Parts of your journal may be a set of index cards; a ring-binder; a cardboard box; a filing cabinet; a Dictaphone; or the backs of envelopes. Don't get too hung up on the idea of your journal as an attractive hard-backed book with creamy vellum pages. Your journal lives where it emerges.

Much of the writing you do is pressurized. If you are writing a novel or a screenplay, you do so under the pressure of keeping the narrative tense and moving forward. One of the joys of journal writing is that it allows you to be completely free. Anything may happen in your journal. Nobody need ever read what you write there. It's a place where you may play or experiment. But crucially, your journal is where you write every day and if you are not writing every day you will not be prepared for when you sit down to create an original piece of work for public consumption. If you are not writing every day, in at least one sense you are not a writer, for writers are people who write. That's worth remembering. *RG*

Writing ideas

Take a notebook and go to your nearest railway station. Choose a destination no more than half an hour away, one which you have never been to before. Spend one to two hours in this place and complete these three exercises:

1. *Recording place*
   Record the sights and sounds and smells of a particular location there (a café, a shop, a park). Try to use more than one sense; most of the time most of us limit our writing to what we have seen. Go beyond this.
2. *Recording incident*
   As Nathaniel Hawthorne did, record something happening in this place (I mean the town or area you have gone to, not the specific location of Exercise 1.) The event needn't be as dramatic as Hawthorne's. It might be no more than lovers meeting each other outside a shop.
3. *A week with your journal*
   For one week, use your journal to collect snippets of material towards a piece of creative work. This will include an initial idea and then many kinds of development of the idea: thoughts about characters, narrative, form; snippets of language you encounter and want to incorporate into the work; notes on stories or poems you read and the specific virtues you want to emulate in them. By the end of the week you ought to have a project you feel excited about.

Further reading

Bell, Julia and Paul Magrs (eds), *The Creative Writing Coursebook* (London: Macmillan, 2001).

Oates, Joyce Carol (ed.), *Telling Stories: An Anthology for Writers* (New York: W.W. Norton & Co., 1998).

Rainer, Tristine, *The New Diary: How to Use a Journal for Self-Guidance and Expanded Creativity* (London: Angus and Robertson, 1986).

journey

Journeys and **stories**, as both experience and idea, are tangled together in our culture, interconnected threads stitched into language, so closely, so inextricably, that journey almost always becomes story, story becomes journey. This productive and interactive symbiosis reaches far back in time to the very beginnings of human history. People were surely recounting their treks and adventures – actual and imaginary – long before writing was invented.

The word 'journey' comes from the old French word: *journée* – meaning 'a day', or 'a day's travelling', and many writers have used this idea to structure a **narrative**. A famous example is Alexander Solzhenitsyn's *One Day in the Life of Ivan Denisovitch*, published in 1962, which details the day of a prisoner in a Stalinist labour camp in Siberia and which contributed to the fall of the Soviet Union. More recently, in Ian McEwan's novel *Saturday*, Henry Perowne, the main character, makes criss-cross tracks through London on 15 February 2003, the day of the huge anti-Iraq war march.

For a fiction writer, the journey as plot is a gift. It has its own built-in linear structure: there must be a **beginning**, a setting out; movement from place to place; dramatic encounters on the way; and, finally, some kind of arrival, an **ending**. Many of the oldest and most familiar myths and stories are structured as journeys: Homer's *Odyssey*; *Red Riding Hood*; *On the Road* by Jack Kerouac. In these quest myths the protagonist travels through the world in order to discover something valuable: home, God, wealth, the White Rabbit, love, meaning, truth. Each stage of the journey is a step on the path, a chapter of the story.

The idea of the journey can also be linked to the idea of a life: birth and childhood at the beginning; adulthood in the middle; old age and death at the end. Bunyan's *Pilgrim's Progress* is an allegorical version of this trope – the pilgrim travelling a perilous path towards heaven or hell. Many biographies and autobiographies also rely on this metaphorical structure: in her book *Dust Tracks on a Road*, Zora Neale Hurston describes herself as a pilgrim, and speaks of her early longing to 'walk out to the horizon'.

Since Darwin and Einstein, many of us are uncomfortably aware that human history may only be a brief flicker in the eye of the universe, that space/time is far more weird and complex than we are able to imagine and that time may not always flow in the usual direction. Martin Amis's novel *Time's Arrow* begins at the end of a man's life and takes us back to the beginning, and Alexander Masters' dramatic biography of a homeless man,

Stuart, A Life Backwards, uses the same device to show how Stuart came to be in such a desperate state.

The writing process itself is often likened to a journey and perhaps it isn't surprising that a large number of how-to-write books draw on this idea. Christopher Vogel's *The Writer's Journey* is one of the best-known, using the psychological philosophies of Carl Jung and the mythological studies of Joseph Campbell to argue that all stories, including the story of the struggling writer, are structured in this archetypal way. The linear life-as-pilgrimage plot may be a gift to writers, but there is a risk that, followed as writing-by-numbers, it could become over-rationalized, producing predictable and clichéd journeys which will only lead us to places we've already been. In her poem, 'The Writer on, and at, Her Work', Ursula le Guin describes the experience of writing as 'walking: on a path through a pathless forest/ or a maze, a labyrinth' (Le Guin, in Sternburg, 1992, p. 154). Here the journey is unpredictable, *pathless*, both line *and* maze.   *HL*

Writing ideas

Imagine a present-day character setting out on a path into a dark and risky place where she/he will meet challenge and adventure, and from which she/he may or may not return safely. The journey should be set in the present day – for example, a visit to the bank to ask for a loan; the first day on a new job or course; a visit home after a long time away.

Keep the key quest elements in the story: setting out; encountering dangers; overcoming difficulties; reaching the end of the journey; but transform these into contemporary experience, and allow the unexpected, the unpredictable, to happen – both to the character and to you, on your own writer's path.

Further reading

Amis, Martin, *Time's Arrow* (London: Vintage, 2003).

Hurston, Zora Neale, *Dust Tracks on a Road* (London: HarperCollins, 1996).

Masters, Alexander, *Stuart, A Life Backwards* (London: Harper Perennial, 2006).

Solzhenitsyn, Alexander, *One Day in the Life of Ivan Denisovitch* (London: Prentice Hall, 2004).

Sternburg, Janet, *The Writer on Her Work* (London: Virago, 1992).

Vogel, Christopher, *The Writer's Journey* (London: Pan, 1999).

language

Language is the writer's medium, the stuff we make into fiction, poetry, drama. There are a thousand metaphors that could be used to illustrate this point: just as the potter manipulates clay, so writers shape the language; as the furniture-maker planes and polishes wood, so the writer . . . you get the idea. These images may be over-worn but they are useful ways of thinking about the writer's relationship to language. For example, the potter and the carpenter need to know about the properties of their chosen material, its differences and variations, care and treatment, origins, traditions and history. So far, so similar; but there are interesting limitations to these comparisons.

The most obvious is that language use is not confined to a specialist few but acquired by almost all human beings from infancy onwards. We appear to be the only creatures on the planet with a systematic linguistic system and even people with hearing or speech disabilities are able to develop full and complex sign languages. Language is one of the key attributes that define us as human. There are many theories about how this came about. Steven Pinker, for example, the psycholinguist, argues that language ability is hardwired into our biology, a basic human instinct which evolved like other biological adaptations (Pinker, 1995). Others argue that language is cultural rather than biological, learned behaviour rather than instinctive. Despite the debates, we still have no definitive theory of how language developed in our ape-like ancestors, or even how the brain makes language possible.

Wittgenstein said that 'the limits of my language mean the limits of my world' (1992, p. 148). If we do not have a word for something, we cannot imagine it, cannot discuss it, cannot think about it, and some people would even argue that if you can't name something, you can't experience it at all.

We are born into language, into the world already named and described by parents, teachers, books, advertisers, governments, priests and websites. Our feelings and ideas, understanding and values, are formed when we are young, by the very words we think we control. Language *shapes us*.

Language is power, as dictators and political leaders know well. Books are regularly banned and even burned. In his essay 'Politics and the English Language', George Orwell points out that a limited vocabulary and weak control of the language means that we are unable to think clearly and are vulnerable to ignorance and manipulation. In the former Yugoslavia in the 1990s, the euphemistic term 'ethnic cleansing' was used by the Serb aggressors to describe the forced eviction, murder and attempted genocide of Bosnian Muslims. Military authorities speak of *collateral damage* when referring to civilian casualties. 'If thought corrupts language, language can also corrupt thought', said Orwell. This is important for everybody to think about but crucial for writers, and Orwell's essay is a good place to start.

Language may be our material but for many people language learning becomes solely identified with technical detail: **grammar** and **punctuation**, etc. Technical skills are important but so too is curiosity and playfulness. It is necessary to know most of the basic rules so that you can effectively communicate and also so that you will know how to skilfully break the rules when necessary. However, more important than technical perfection is a playful and attentive *feeling* for language, for the right word in the right place, the swing of a sentence, for pattern and rhythm, for the way language endlessly moves and shifts between people, between cultures, through time. Make language say what you want it to say – and let it speak through you.

HL

Further reading

Orwell, George, 'Politics and The English Language', in *Essays* (London: Penguin, 2000); also at www.george-orwell.org/Politics_and_the_English_Language/0.html.
Pinker, Steven, *The Language Instinct* (London: Penguin, 1995).
Wittgenstein, Ludwig, *Tractatus Logico-philosophicus* (London: Routledge, 1992).

learning

Whether you study it at college or university or on your own in your **garret**, learning how to write is going to take a long time. Thomas Pynchon once published a collection of his early work which he called *Slow Learner*. That's about the height of it. Nobody learns how to write quickly. Learning is connected to studying – examining the work of writers you admire and taking it to pieces to see how they've done it – but it's also connected to graft and output: the more you write, the more your writing will develop.

RG

length

In higher education, Creative Writing students are often to be overheard bemoaning the length of an assignment and the limitations that having to stick to it has placed them under. 'If I'd had 2,000 words instead of 1,000, I could really have pulled this story off', etc. Stuff and nonsense. It's in learning to write to length that you are forced to develop. The alternative, setting you off to write a 3,000-word story first time out, would only be giving you enough rope with which to hang yourself. Another angle on this is that, in the real world, you will be constrained by length. Competitions have set word lengths and if you try submitting a 300,000-word novel, nobody will want to look at it.   *RG*

library

The old stereotype of the library was a place where you got shouted at if you made a noise; the staff were dried-up spinsters except for the beautiful girls with glasses and bad hairdos, waiting for romantic rescue. Of course, this was always jock propaganda but the image is hard to shake off. Today most libraries are noisy places: information points; meeting spaces; computer resource centres; multimedia hire shops. This is mainly a good thing, creating wider access. But we do need to remember that libraries are also about BOOKS. You can sit and read for as long as they're open. You can wander the shelves, just looking and browsing. You can reserve books from a much greater stock. You can do all this in bookshops as well, the only disadvantage being that you also have to part with cash, whereas you or yours have already paid for the library through taxes or fees. You'd miss it if it wasn't there.   *HL*

lineation

Literally, the act of making a line or drawing with lines. The art of lineation helps to differentiate poetry from other genres: whereas most prose runs along the page from left to right, poets have the freedom to decide where to begin and end their lines and how to separate them into stanzas (aka verses).

Traditional poetry consists of stanzas named according to the number of lines: couplets (2); tercets (3); quatrains (4), cinquains (5), sestets (6), septets (7) and octaves (8). The left margin is usually justified, but the right-hand line-breaks should be carefully constructed, paying close attention to punctuation. Poets make use of devices such as 'enjambment', in which the sentence and/or sense runs over the end of the line; 'end-stopped lines', in which the sense or sentence ceases with the end of the line; and 'caesura', in which a pause is created in the middle of the line via punctuation or spacing. Enjambment and caesura create rhythm, fluidity and diversity in the poem.

Imagine a poem in which every line is a complete sentence – the only successful example of this I know is Tom Leonard's 'The Psychiatrist' in which the tedium of sitting in a shrink's office, waiting for your hour to be up is evoked! In all other cases, the end-stopped line (like the one-word sentence or line) should be used sparingly and for emphasis. This sets a scene, but also raises more questions than it answers. The same considerations apply to the transition between one stanza and another: you need to decide how and whether to run the sentence on. Next time you look at a poem, try to trace the poet's lineation and consider why they have structured their poem as they have. The crucial thing to remember is that you are working with a specialized form of poetic grammar involving punctuation, lineation and stanza structure. *HT*

Further reading

Leonard, Tom, *Intimate Voices: Selected Work 1965–1983* (London: Vintage, 1995).

Herbert, W. N., in Linda Anderson, *Creative Writing: A Workbook with Readings* (London: Routledge, 2005).

love

Permeates the act of writing in all its forms. Writers need to be in love with writing:

> The secret of the thing that consoles is that it can be relied upon: the walk will always be there, the faithful dog, the garden in all its seasons, will be there, and writing's the same, it will always be there, the story you're telling. (Tremain, 2002)

You do it because you can't not, because it dominates your waking hours and haunts your dreams. We crave the endorphin hit that the act of creation gives us. As Charles Bukowski says in his poem 'Writing',

> often it is the only
> thing
> between you and

love

> impossibility.
> no drink,
> no woman's love,
> no wealth
> can
> match it. (Bukowski, 2004, p. 225)

So that's *why* we do it, but when we do it, what do we write about? Most successful works of literature concern love in some way or other: romantic love, family love, friendship or comradeship. In fact it's almost impossible to think of a story that doesn't have love in some form as a theme. Love is probably as close as we can get to a universal concept and this makes it an absolute gift for the creative writer. All plots need a driving force, all characters need motivation. Love provides these things in bucketfuls. If one character loves another, then they will stop at nothing to communicate that love, whether that takes the form of saving their beloved from a monster, or seeking their hand in marriage.

Although almost every human being in the world has experienced love in some way or other, trying to capture the nuances of that feeling in words has always been hugely difficult. The fourteenth-century Persian poet Hafiz wrote: 'Words have no language which can utter the secrets of love'. Shakespeare got close with his sonnets, and legions of subsequent writers have had a crack at it. The challenge for any writer wishing to address a grand theme like love is to avoid descending into the pink mush of cliché. How do we articulate this emotion in a credible, engaging way? Anthropologist Robin Allott offers a useful approach:

> Human love as we experience it, as it is reported and manifested, is essentially a relation between one person and another. (Allott, 1992, p. 353)

The way people relate to each other, the way they interact, is of course a rich vein for a writer. We don't need to have a character navel-gazing (which is usually rather boring for the reader) in order to signal his or her emotions. We can show it in the way they speak and the way they behave. It doesn't matter if we can't describe love itself: as long as we can capture its manifestations, our readers can tap into their own experiences of this difficult, slippery, wonderful emotion.   *UH*

Writing ideas

Feels like I'm in love

Make a list of the kinds of things people in love do (e.g. staring into space, smiling at nothing, jumping in puddles). Now write a scene which involves a character in love. Have your character do some or all of the things on your list in order to show rather than describe their feelings.

Further reading

Tremain, Rose, interviewed in *Mslexia*, 15 (2002) (www.mslexia.co.uk/interview/extract15.html, accessed 13 December 2006).

Bukowski, Charles, *The Flash of Lightning Behind the Mountain* (New York: Ecco, 2004).

Hafiz of Shiraz, c.1326–90, www.thesongsofhafiz.com (accessed 13 December 2006).

Allott, Robin, 'Evolutionary Aspects of Love and Empathy', *Journal of Social and Evolutionary Systems*, 15 (4), pp. 353–70 (Oxford: Elsevier, 1992).

lyric

The ancient Greek lyric gave birth to contemporary poetry. Its characteristics include musicality (it was originally sung to the accompaniment of the lyre), emotion and use of 'I', all of which are still commonly associated with poetry. The most interesting ancient lyric poet is Sappho, translated by many modern poets and scholars. Her fragments are highly suggestive, often providing a springboard for original work. One contemporary poet who explores the conventions of lyric is Denise Riley.   *HT*

Further reading

Balmer, Josephine, *Sappho Poems and Fragments* (London: Brilliance Books, 1984).

Riley, Denise, *Selected Poems* (London: Reality Street Editions, 2000).

magic realism

As the name suggests, a form of contemporary fiction, often associated with South American and post-colonial writers, that mixes fantastical and magical elements with realistic narrative. Characters in magic realist stories are visited by angels, speak with animals, read minds, and ascend, still alive, into heaven. A key aspect of magic realism is hybridity: the merging and clashing of elements which are usually separate or opposed; the crossing of boundaries, natural and supernatural, masculine and feminine, urban and rural.

Magic realist writers, including Isabel Allende, Gabriel Garcia Marquez and Salman Rushdie, use the form to explore complex political and social issues, such as colonialism and feminism, in ways that avoid preachy social-realism. A key challenge for the writer is how to make the boundaries between the real and the magical disappear.   *HL*

Further reading
Allende, Isabel, *The House of the Spirits* (London: Black Swan, 1994).
Marquez, Gabriel Garcia, *One Hundred Years of Solitude* (London: Penguin, 1998).

manuscript

The somewhat antiquated term for the draft of the book which you send to your agent and then on to the publishers. The term implies that it is hand-written when it is more likely to be word-processed these days, i.e. a typescript. The typescript can be a hard copy or can be a word-processed data file, CD, or – increasingly the case – an email attachment.

Make sure that your typescript has a face sheet detailing your name and address, contact details, the title, a description of what it is, and a word count. Also make sure that the typescript is sent to your agent or publisher in a form that suits them – for example, telephone them to ask if they prefer electronic scripts and, if so, which software or format they prefer.

The industry standard for a typescript is that they are double-spaced, page-numbered, with wide margins, and have an unobtrusive header or footer with a summary description of author and title. It is essential that the script is clean and professionally presented. Common pitfalls are failure to provide accurate spelling, grammar and paragraph indenting. Although publishers are always looking for the next J. K. Rowling or Zadie Smith, they will use a sloppy typescript as a short cut to reducing the size of their slush pile. Don't give them the opportunity. GC

memory

What exactly is memory? The dictionary definition says: 'the faculty by which the mind stores and remembers information' (*Concise OED*, 11th edn), which is fair enough, probably the way most of us would define it, until you begin to question what is meant by the terms: *mind, store* and *information*. The unwritten assumption behind this very rational and familiar definition is that the mind is like a large computer which collects knowledge, learning and experience, and neatly files it away into well-organized (unconscious) spaces inside the head, bringing bits out into conscious memory only when required. Except that, as we all know, it isn't as simple as that.

If the mind is like a computer, it's full of bugs. We forget a great deal; we remember only in pieces and patches. Different people remember the same events differently, and some memories may even be completely false. Contemporary research shows that memory may work in a similar way to fiction, constructing narratives out of fragmentary experience. If this is true, then it may help to explain why we are so addicted to stories: making them up may be one of the mind's primary functions. HL

(See **autobiography**)

Further reading

Fireman, Gary, Owen Flanagan and Ted McVay, *Narrative and Consciousness: Literature, Psychology, and the Brain* (Oxford: Oxford University Press, 2002).

metafiction

Fiction which is about fiction. This can be simply a story with a writer as the main protagonist, but the term mainly refers to work which is self-consciously reflexive, breaking the frame of the realist illusion. This may be through direct authorial intervention, as in John Fowles' 1969 historical novel *The French Lieutenant's Woman*, which includes commentary on research as well as discussion of the writing process and two possible endings. See also much of Robert Coover's work, in particular his short story 'The Magic Poker', where the narrator is character and author, both god-like creators:

> I wander the island, inventing it. I make a sun for it and trees – pines and birch and dogwood and firs – and cause the water to lap the pebbles of its abandoned shores. (Coover, 1989, p. 14)

HL

(See **postmodernism**)

Further reading

Coover, Robert, 'The Magic Poker', in *Pricksongs and Descants* (London: Minerva, 1989).

Fowles, John, *The French Lieutenant's Woman* (London: Penguin, 1969).

metaphor

A figure of speech or **image** which connects two normally unconnected things to create a vivid impression: the car engine coughs; she is my comfort blanket. Metaphors can be extended, as in Shakespeare's series of theatrical images from *As You Like It*:

> All the world's a stage
> And all the men and women merely players:
> They have their exits and their entrances. (II, 7, 139–41)

As well as the use of worn-out metaphors, which may be **clichés**, the common metaphorical pitfall for writers is the mixed metaphor, which joins two or more images to create an inappropriate or ludicrous effect: *you are my cast-iron comfort blanket; he took the road map to peace through a tidal wave of political fallout.* There's a lot more to metaphor than its use as literary image. As Guy Deutscher says in *The Unfolding of Language*, 'Metaphor is the essential tool of thought . . . the only way we have of dealing with abstraction.' (Deutscher, 2006, p. 142)   *HL*

(See **imagery; simile**)

Further reading

Deutscher, Guy, *The Unfolding of Language* (London: Random House Arrow, 2006).

metonymy

Metonymy focuses on the contiguity between things that are naturally close to each other. An example of metonymy is the synecdoche in which the part is substituted for the whole – for instance, crown for queen. Metonymy is generally seen as less flashy and more organic than **metaphor**.   *HT*

metre and rhythm

All language has rhythm: we can hear it in everyday speech and feel it in good prose. Poetry makes a special feature of rhythm. Sometimes this is a free-verse rhythm invented by the poet in order to create mood and musicality in each individual poem. Free-verse poetry works with the natural stresses in the language and with the rhythm of the human breath in order to create an organic rhythm. Two poets well worth reading in this context are D. H. Lawrence and Lee Harwood.

Metre is the rhythm of a poem as defined by the pattern of stresses (aka accents or emphases). The discipline of analysing metre is called prosody. It breaks up lines into numbers of strong and weak stresses and then calculates that each line has, for instance, five weak and five strong stresses, with the weak ones coming first. Traditionally, poets mainly wrote in set metres, but today it is rarer, although still in evidence. The twentieth-century American poet Robert Frost was famous for his adherence to metre. Here is a line from his superb poem 'The Most of It': 'And *noth*ing *ever came* of *what* he *cried*'. You may recognize this as an iambic pentameter, with each unit of unstressed/stressed syllable being described as an iamb (a type of metrical 'foot'). This pattern of stresses, with the unstressed beat coming first, echoes the beating of the human heart (de *dum*, de *dum*, de *dum*) or the tick of a clock (tick *tock*, tick *tock*, tick *tock*). Perhaps this is why poets skilled in the use of metre can manipulate iambs to make them sound like natural speech.

Whatever kind of poem you are reading or writing, the important thing is to be able to hear the stresses in a line. You can do this by sounding the words aloud syllable by syllable, increasing emphasis and volume on the strong stresses. Practice on familiar nursery rhymes with a strong beat, such as '*Pol*ly *put* the *ket*tle *on*'.

If you do work with metre, remember that the greatest poets always bend the rules to make the rhythm more interesting. Even Frost worked in plenty of intentional slips which make his poems more subtle and evocative. If you *don't* want to employ set metres, remember that all poets need to create a beat in their work, however irregular, and that all language consists of stressed and unstressed syllables.   *HT*

Writing ideas
* Pick up a book by a 'poetic' prose writer (say Virginia Woolf);
* choose a long sentence that appeals to you;
* spread the sentence over three or four lines and scan it (you and Woolf have now created a metre);
* write another stanza whose metre mirrors the first exactly (and another?).

Further reading
Frost, Robert, *Poems* (New York: St Martin's Paperbacks, 2002).

Harwood, Lee, *Collected Poems* (Exeter: Shearsman, 2004).

Hobsbaum, Philip, *Metre, Rhythm and Verse Form* (London: Routledge, 1996).

Lawrence, D. H., *Selected Poems* (London: Penguin, 2005).

Roberts, Philip Davies, *How Poetry Works* (London, Penguin, 1991).

middle
Where the main action of the story happens. Chekhov suggested writing the beginning, middle and end, then cutting the beginning and the end. All very well, but often the beginning and the end can be easier to write than the bit between them. In the middle, conflict should be intensifying. However, in the middle, the plot may flag or sag; the author may lose her way. In terms of dramatic fiction, the middle is where the **protagonist** faces increased pressure from the forces of opposition, is faced with defeat and finds ways to overcome. See? Couldn't be easier.   *RG*

modernism
This is linked with, but (confusingly) not the same as, the word *modern*. 'Modern' relates to newness and the present, whether referring to 1066 or 2006. 'Modern*ism*' refers to a particular historical period at the beginning of the twentieth century, a period which saw radical movements in arts and culture, including literature. Many modernists rejected the **Romantic** emphasis on the rural as well as the rational realism of the Victorians, focusing instead on the city, on the inner life of the individual, and, after the First World War, on a more pessimistic view of human society. Modernist writers experimented with open forms; precise imagery; free verse, fractured poetic narrative as in T. S. Eliot's *The Waste Land*, and

stream of consciousness. If you are interested in the history of experimentation, read the modernists.   *HL*

(See **postmodernism**)

Further reading
Eliot, T. S., *The Waste Land, Prufrock and Other Poems* (London: Penguin, 2003).

money
Some writers consider money to be a great motivator but this is unlikely to have a positive effect on your output. Writing has to be from the heart and generally speaking it is difficult to write outside the genre in which you are most genuinely interested. Therefore, how much money you are likely to make will be determined by the form and genre within which you write. That is to say, a successful existential poet will probably earn less from their writing than their thriller novelist counterpart.

Money in publishing can be a good and a bad thing. Good because the thought of it gets you out of bed; and also, the more they give you, the harder your publisher has to try to sell your books. Money is also the most accurate barometer of whether you are pleasing your audience. Money can be bad because it is very, very seldom enough to live on without having to do something else and it can also measure your (lack of) success.

Basically, if you are successful, money is a good thing. This makes writers indistinguishable from builders, musicians, shopkeepers and anyone outside of the public sector. The lack of money lends a certain bohemian lustre to the writer's life and gives the fashionably obscure something to moan to each other about.   *GC*

monologue
A long speech, often spoken by an actor as part of a play, but sometimes as a stand-alone performance. A monologue can also be a passage from a novel or short story in which a character's thoughts are presented in direct speech or as interior monologue. This can include all the character's inner life, a **stream of consciousness**: impressions, images, feelings, thoughts and ideas. Monologues can also be written as if the characters are talking to themselves: re-running the past, planning the future, justifying their actions, etc.

Some monologues are autobiographical. Spalding Gray used his often painful experiences to construct dramatic performances. He described writing and performing as 'a form of oral writing . . . storytelling your own life' (Gray, Interview with Liza Weisstuch, *Harvard University Gazette*, 17 January 2001. See full interview at: www.news.harvard.edu/gazette/2002/01.17/03-gray.html.)

However, a monologue is not simply a voice but a shaped narrative, a story, even if the story is no more than the revelation of character. Alan Bennett's monologue series, *Talking Heads*, originally written for television, includes a range of characters: an actress in a porn movie; a closet homosexual; the alcoholic wife of a vicar. Each has a distinctive voice but a number of Bennett's narrators are struggling with conflicts and passions which are only half-conscious, unreliable witnesses to their own lives. One of the key elements of an effective monologue is the particularity of the voice speaking – the rhythms, vocabulary and register of that person in that situation. The best way to develop skills in this area is to listen to people talking.

HL

Writing ideas
1. Imagine a difficult situation – for example:
   - being stuck in mud for three days. (This actually happened recently. A jogger out for a half-hour run got stuck just out of yelling distance of his place of work. Only Samuel Beckett could make it up!);
   - knowing a secret that would cause pain if it was revealed;
   - being obsessed with another person.
2. Imagine the character whose story this is: note down brief details of their life so far, likes and dislikes, habits and interests.
3. Decide who the person is talking to: themselves (an inner voice); another person; the reader/audience. Now let the character speak. Set the monologue in three short scenes with pauses in between. Scene one: situation/character are revealed. Scene two: situation develops/character changes, understands more, and makes a decision. Scene three: resolution.

Further reading
Bennett, Alan, *Talking Heads* (London: BBC, 1997). Text, audio and video.
Gray, Spalding, *Gray's Anatomy* (London: Picador, 1993).

multiple viewpoint
Fiction with more than one **point of view** (POV). When there are only two point of view characters, it's called dual viewpoint. The trouble with dual

viewpoint is that readers will almost always prefer one POV to the other. In single viewpoint, they don't have a choice; they either like the narrator or put the book away. The benefit of more than one point of view is that you escape the chief limitation of single viewpoint – that your **narrator** has to witness everything. If you have several viewpoint characters, you are even less limited. A change of viewpoint character also offers variety and gives the reader a rest from the previous narrator. Remember, though, that a single narrator offers a more cohesive experience for the reader. It's possible to fall in love with the narrator in a single viewpoint novel (for instance, Holden Caulfield in *The Catcher in the Rye*). In a multiple viewpoint work, it's a lot less likely.   *RG*

names

Names have power. Many cultural traditions believe that to know someone's name is to have dominance over them. Fiction writers need to consider carefully the names they give to their characters. Fashions change over time: for example, someone aged 20 is unlikely to be called Ethel today, and the name Tracy wasn't used until the 1960s. Some names take on the mood and tone of the story as they become familiarized in culture: Hamlet is synonymous with indecision, Carrie with horror. Others seem absolutely fixed, as if the character could never have been called anything else: Doctor Who; Cinderella; Darth Vader; Harry Potter. Many writers use names to suggest character: Dickens' awful teacher was Gradgrind; Doris Lessing's woman on a journey was Martha Quest. Some names are made up: Nosmo King was the stage name of an American comedian, and Max Headroom the name of a character in a television show. Both names were derived from well-known public signs and you could try and make up one or two of your own from similar sources, inventing a character to go with the name. It's useful to have a name book beside you, the kind prospective parents buy. *HL*

Further reading

Dunkling, Leslie, *The Guinness Book of Names* (London: Guinness Publishing, 1991).

narrative

A sequence of causally related events. The king died and then the queen died is not a narrative. However, the king died and then the queen died of a broken heart is. As a result of the first thing, the second thing happened. Causality. But more demands on the events that may constitute a narrative are required. Ansen Dibell develops this point about causality and emphasizes the importance of significance:

Plot is the things characters do, feel, think, or say, that make a difference to what comes afterward. (Dibell, 1990, p. 6)

This connects with Alfred Hitchcock's observation that drama is life with the dull parts removed. Any old events will not make a narrative. Not only must they be causally related, but they will also need to have sufficient dramatic significance to carry your characters and your readers along. A novel-length narrative is unlikely to be constructed from descriptions of housework. Just a quick glance at my bookshelf shows novels about the murder of a dog; the sufferings of two generations of Chinese women; the trials the family of an alcoholic goes through; and the fire-bombing of Dresden in 1945.

A narrative is a sequence of dramatic, causally related events which takes both characters and readers on a journey. Implicit in this definition is the notion of *change*. A narrative must involve change.

A narrative which works will engage its readers and this is achieved through three interrelated concepts: intrigue, suspense and tension. Intrigue is a matter of creating a question in the mind of the reader. A story might begin: *I wasn't going to fall for that.* Immediately, at least two questions have been lodged in the reader's mind. What was it that the narrator wasn't going to fall for? Why was the narrator not going to fall for it? A third is possible, too: Who was this other person trying to trick the narrator and why? Suspense is when the reader wonders what is going to happen and has to wait to find out. In the novel I'm reading at the moment, the protagonist warns people in the village he arrives in that he is being pursued by a cannibal. I'm in suspense about when this cannibal is going to show up and what will happen when he does. Suspense that works has an element of tension to it. Had the protagonist shown up in a village and said he was being pursued by an insurance salesman, I doubt my suspense would have been so tense. Suspense also concerns the reader being kept waiting to find out the answers to all the questions you prompt.

Tension may be generated by intrigue or suspense, but probably the most common engine of narrative tension is conflict, which you should now add to your growing list of essential elements of a narrative. (For James N. Frey's helpful advice, see **conflict**.) Conflict may arise from characters disagreeing, or having different responses to a crisis. Conflict may well be internal: a character wanting to do one thing and doing another or trying to come to terms with two opposing impulses. Whatever the nature of the conflict you choose, it is not the conflict in itself that generates your narrative, it is the

narrative

way your character responds to that conflict. In *One Flew Over The Cuckoo's Nest*, R. P. McMurphy isn't the only person suffering under Big Nurse's regime on that psychiatric ward, but it's the way he responds to being in that situation that generates the narrative of Kesey's novel.

In constructing a plot that includes as much as possible of the above – from causality to steadily rising conflict – a useful litmus test is to ask yourself this simple question: What's at stake? If the answer is 'Will Jack's spot be ready to squeeze by morning?' you may well deduce that this is not enough. If, on the other hand, the answer to that question is, 'Will Rosie survive now that she has a new boss who appears hell-bent on getting rid of her?' you probably have a viable narrative under way.

Now that we have had a look at what narrative might be, it's time to give some thought to how you actually produce one. Anne Lamott speaks of 'flail[ing] around, *kvetching* and growing despondent, on the way to finding a plot and structure that work' (Lamott, 1995, p. 55). In other words, it's not easy. Do you begin by planning? Many fiction writers claim not to, although it seems that crime writers often do. Do you set off without a plan of any kind? Most writers appear not to. However, there seems to be a consensus that setting off with some characters and a loose plan and then writing to discover is preferable. A great deal of writing on the subject suggests that the unconscious mind has access to the source of narratives. Many writers think of a story as something which already exists somewhere in the unconscious. Accessing it and recording it is then a matter of knowing how best to tap the unconscious mind (see **creativity**). 'Plot', says Ashley Stokes, 'is part of the process of writing. It is something we find in the activity itself' (in Bell and Magrs, 2001, p. 207). Perhaps the best argument for writing to discover is that if you have your narrative all planned out and know what is going to happen, how fulfilling is it going to be to write? Are you a copy typist or a writer? If you write without fully knowing what is going to happen, you are at any given point in the construction of the narrative putting yourself in a similar position to the reader, which is bound to be helpful, since understanding how the reader perceives the story is half the battle in constructing a narrative. As you flail and *kvetch*, remember E. L. Doctorow's simile:

> Writing a novel is like driving a car at night. You can only see as far as your headlights, but you can make the whole trip that way. (in Lamott, 1995, p. 18)

RG

Writing ideas

1. *Intrigue*

   Write an intriguing opening line for a story – stimulus: a secret. (For example: *I racked my brains trying to remember where I had lost it.*) Now write the first page of this story, which must feature two further pieces of intrigue.

2. *Causality*

   Write a 500-word narrative in which one thing leads to another which leads to a third thing. The emphasis is on cause and effect: because *this* happened, *this* happened. Stimulus: a betrayal.

3. *Steadily rising conflict*

   Write another 500-word narrative – stimulus: an elderly couple who are fed up with one another – in which the conflict, the tension between the couple, rises steadily.

Further reading

Dibell, Ansen, *Plot* (London: Robinson Publishing, 1990).

Lamott, Anne, *Bird By Bird – Some Instructions on Writing and Life* (New York: Anchor Books, 1995).

Stokes, Ashley, 'Plotting A Novel' in Julia Bell and Paul Magrs (eds), *The Creative Writing Coursebook* (London: Macmillan, 2001).

narrative tension

The factor in a story which will keep readers turning the page or viewers watching. Principally, narrative tension is created by **conflict**. When readers or viewers are in a state of suspense about what will happen to the narrator, you have successfully generated narrative tension. The kind of tension you want to create comes from steadily rising conflict. Narrative tension will build satisfyingly for your reader as life gradually gets more difficult for your **protagonist**.   *RG*

narrator

The person who tells the story. More often than not, the narrator is the **point of view** character. (The exception is when there is an **omniscient narrator**.) The narrator and the protagonist may be one and the same, but often the narrator is an observer, and the protagonist his principal subject. The narrator is in a relationship between the protagonist, the story and the reader, and the distance between any of these aspects may increase or decrease. The story, for instance, may be happening now, in which the distance between narrator and story is very small; or at some time in the past, in which case the distance is greater.

The narrator is usually trustworthy but some are unreliable. According to David Lodge, the point of using an unreliable narrator is 'to reveal in an interesting way the gap between appearance and reality, and to show how human beings distort or conceal the latter' (Lodge, 1992, p. 155). Trustworthy or reliable, villainous or heroic, your narrator should be so charming as to entice the reader into a close relationship.   *RG*

Further reading
Lodge, David, *The Art of Fiction* (London: Penguin, 1992).

non-fiction

Prose that has not been made up, such as **autobiography**. On the face of it. Of course, a good deal of fiction is based on fact, and a good deal of non-fiction includes fictional elements. In American universities, they teach Literary Non-Fiction, part of which is something called the Non-Fiction Short Story. The thinking behind this is applying the techniques of fiction to writing non-fiction, something that goes back to Truman Capote's non-fiction novel *In Cold Blood*.   *RG*

notebooks

Devices for collecting ideas and material. The principal reason for carrying a notebook is so that you can record your ideas when you get them because if you don't, they will be lost. Implicit in this is the fact that we don't only get ideas for work in progress when we are sitting at a keyboard. The notebook is also useful for recording overheard conversations (see **eavesdropping**) and for practising when you have a few spare moments. John Fowles spoke of this as being like bar exercises for ballet dancers and said of his habit of keeping journals and notebooks, 'I think that is how I became a novelist, eventually.'   *RG*
(See also **journals**)

novel

The normal expectations of a novel are that it should be prose, fictional and long. However, there have been novels written in verse (see Vikram Seth's *The Golden Gate*); non-fictional novels (see Truman Capote's *In Cold Blood*); and there are plenty of examples of short works: Charles Dickens' *A*

Christmas Carol; Joseph Conrad's *Heart of Darkness*; George Orwell's *Animal Farm*, although these may also be called *novellas*. The only safe definition is that a novel is longer than a short story (more than 20,000 words) and has book covers all to itself.

A lot of beginning writers ask how long a novel should be, but there is no absolute set of rules. There are many examples of enormous door-stoppers: *The Crimson Petal and The White* by Michael Faber has 848 pages, and perhaps the most famous is *War and Peace* by Leo Tolstoy, weighing in at an astonishing 1,376 pages. Thankfully, most are between 60,000 and 100,000 words long. This variability of form, shape and size is probably the main reason that the novel is still going strong despite many announcements of its imminent death. Another reason for its continuing popularity is that, because of its length, it promises immersivity, the opportunity to live in a different place, to become other selves for a time.

Novels can be light or dark; realistic or fantastic; they can follow a formula or be playfully experimental. There are many sub-genres, sometimes categorized as escapist or popular fiction: crime; sci-fi; horror; fantasy, etc., all with their fans and critics, and these are sometimes unfavourably compared with work defined as 'literary' or 'serious'. Some of these divisions may be useful, helping readers to pick their way through an overwhelming abundance of writers and titles, but some hierarchical comparisons are snobbish and limiting. The important thing for the writer is to read widely and deeply and to remember that what readers are looking for is a *really good read* and that 'good' can have as many different meanings as there are people.

How do you write a novel? There are as many theories as writers. Paddy Kitchen says, 'The best time to embark on the writing is when the idea has been lodged in your mind for some time but you still show no signs of losing interest in it' (Kitchen, 1981, p. 4). You will need this interest to be able to sustain a novel-length draft which may have to be rewritten many times. As you write, you will need to find the story and make it into a shape that works. Emma Tennant speaks of a 'six or seven-year' wrestle with structure, 'accumulating a great heap of unfinished manuscripts under my bed' (Tennant, in Sellers, 1989, p. 27). Nadine Gordimer comments that:

> A novel . . . is staked out, and must be taken possession of stage by stage; it is impossible to contain, all at once, the proliferation of concepts it ultimately may use. (Gordimer, 1989, p. 117)

novel

Writing a novel is a journey without satnav or roadmap: exciting but with lots of wrong turns and dead ends. Fortunately, if you are still determined to set out, there are many excellent guides.   *HL*

Further reading

Capote, Truman, *In Cold Blood* (London: Penguin, 1993).

Conrad, Joseph, *Heart of Darkness* (London: Penguin, 1994).

Dickens, Charles, *A Christmas Carol* (London: Wordsworth, 1993).

Faber, Michael, *The Crimson Petal and The White* (London: Canongate, 2003).

Gordimer, Nadine, *The Essential Gesture* (London: Penguin, 1989).

Grenville, Kate, *The Writing Book* (London: Allen and Unwin, 1990).

Kitchen, Paddy, *The Way to Write Novels* (London: Elm Tree Books, 1981).

Orwell, George, *Animal Farm* (London: Penguin, 1996).

Seth, Vikram, *The Golden Gate* (London: Faber, 1999).

observation

Paying close attention. According to William Trevor, 'the only way you can create a character is through observation' (Plimpton, 1999, p. 203). I would suggest that the same is equally true of the creation of setting. Like your thoughts, there is a sense in which what you witness does not fully exist for you until you have expressed it in writing. What you observe in writing is a record not only of what you see (and hear and smell) but also of the person you were and the situation you were in when you were doing the observing. Also, recording something in writing as you witness it gives it a freshness that writing about it at a later point will not have. You have written a report on location, not a reminiscence. *RG*

Further reading

Plimpton, George, *The Writer's Chapbook* (New York: Penguin, 1999).

omniscient narrator

An omniscient narrator witnesses everything that happens in fiction, offering readers a view roughly from the perspective of God. In the eighteenth and nineteenth centuries, the author acting as omniscient narrator was accepted practice. Jane Austen's opening line in *Pride and Prejudice* is a good example of the omniscient tone: 'It is a truth universally acknowledged, that a single man in possession of a good fortune must be in want of a wife.' However, beginning with Chekhov at the end of the nineteenth century, omniscient narrators have largely become unfashionable. James Joyce suggested the desirability of the author remaining offstage 'paring his fingernails'. Jenny Newman (2004) recommends care when using the omniscient form 'because few modern readers like to be lectured'. *RG*

Further reading

Newman, Jenny, Edmund Cusick and Aileen La Tourette (eds), *The Writer's Workbook* (London: Arnold, 2004).

pace

Narrative speed. Several things can enhance the pace of a story. **Narrative tension** (see also **narrative**) will increase pace, as will steadily piling up the pressure on your **protagonist**; there's nothing like raising the stakes in one way or another to enhance both tension and pace. If in doubt, make one thing after another go wrong for your protagonist. In fiction, summary, or telling, will tend to slow the pace whereas scene (or showing) will help to increase it. The rhythm of your sentences will also affect pace. Use short, terse sentences to speed up and longer, layered sentences to slow down. The same is true of paragraphs – at least, it's true to say that short paragraphs will speed up a text. You will often be thinking in terms of increasing pace, but sometimes it's preferable to slow it down – for example, at dramatic moments. Here you want to milk the situation – the car crash where the villain dies or the argument that ends the relationship – for all you're worth, so you slow it down and dwell on the telling details. *RG*

page design

The way your page looks, which is a considerable factor in reader engagement. It would be a shame to fritter away good writing by making your pages unappealing to readers. Page design has to do with the way you lay out text on a page and the effect that has on the reader. Poets know all about this. In earlier times, when society was less visually oriented, readers of fiction could put up with a page which, apart from the space between the lines and between the words, had been filled with text. Today, in the era of the image, readers are less prepared to work their way through monolithic blocks of text. The way advertising, for example, uses text means that we like to see a certain amount of **white space** surrounding words on a page. According to Mike Sharples, 'research suggests that readers prefer text to be set in a more open manner' (Sharples, 1999, p. 139).

The first step towards breaking up the monolith is simple: think carefully about your **paragraphing**. It's possible to get away with paragraphs that run for two to three pages, but this means that your other narrative strategies are having to work harder to compensate for the lack of white space on the page. In narrative prose, you should probably be thinking of two to three paragraphs a page. The openings of stories and chapters benefit from the use of short paragraphs, which will speed the reader into your fiction.

Dialogue creates more white space, because unless your characters are **monologuing** – and bear in mind what happens to super-villains who monologue in *The Incredibles* – dialogue will necessitate a sharp increase in the number of paragraphs per page. If you're interested in pace, dialogue will often consist of short speeches of perhaps only two or three lines each. This will clearly result in more white space.

One contemporary convention is to break chapters and stories down into shorter sections, which are often separate scenes. This is signalled by the use of extra spacing to show that the scene or section is over. **Section-breaks**, like paragraphing and the use of dialogue, will result in more white space on the page.

In her day, Fay Weldon, who before becoming a full-time writer was an advertising copywriter, was innovative in her use of page design. 'Words are given resonance by their positions; they must be displayed properly', she says. 'If you wish to give something emphasis, you surround it by space' (in Haffenden, 1985, pp. 305–20).

If you want to understand the importance of page design in fiction, dig out the densest page you can find in a nineteenth-century novel and compare it to a page from one of Raymond Carver's stories. Which is more inviting?   RG

Further reading

Haffenden, John (ed.), 'Fay Weldon', in *Novelists in Interview* (London: Methuen, 1985), pp. 305–20.
Sharples, Mike, *How We Write* (London: Routledge, 1999), p. 139.

paragraphs

A collection of sentences, perhaps united by their subject matter. Prose breaks down into different lengths of collections of words: sentence, paragraph, section, chapter. As with these other collections of words, paragraphs allow the reader a break, perhaps so that information may be digested. Because of the limits of concentration, but also because of the pressure to create **white space** on the page, paragraphs should arguably be limited in length. Although there are still authors who can get away with paragraphs that run for pages, having at least two to three paragraphs a page is generally regarded as a good idea.

In fiction, paragraphs can be used to help your readers to keep track of what is happening. Taking a new paragraph when there is a new speaker makes accessing dialogue much easier for readers. Similarly, if the focus in a narrative passage shifts from one person to another, taking a new paragraph helps readers see that the focal point of the story has now moved from Character A to Character B.   *RG*

pathetic fallacy

In its most common usage, pathetic fallacy is when the author underscores the emotional content of a scene with the weather: rain when the scene is unhappy, a storm when the couple are having a great argument. However, John Ruskin, who came up with the term, had a different view, declaring that the aim of pathetic fallacy was 'to signify any description of inanimate natural objects that ascribes to them human capabilities, sensations, and emotions' (Ruskin, 1971).   *RG*

Further reading
Ruskin, John, 'Of the Pathetic Fallacy', in *The Aesthetic and Critical Theories of John Ruskin* (Princeton, NJ: Princeton University Press, 1971).

pattern

Echoes and mirrors. Pattern involves creating repetition in much the same way as rolls of wallpaper make use of a repeated image. *Great Expectations* begins with Pip meeting Magwitch in a cemetery and reaches its climax in a cemetery. Lucy Ellman sprinkles her novel *Sweet Desserts* with jokes and recipes. In Kate Mosse's bestseller *Labyrinth*, the characters and situations in the twenty-first-century narrative mirror those in the thirteenth-century narrative. **Plant and pay-off** is another form of pattern.

Pattern is a means of making sense. When the reader comes across the second or third joke in *Sweet Desserts*, he or she can think, 'Ah-ha – I've seen one of these in this novel before. I know what they are.' Pattern may give the reader the impression that he or she is making sense of the text. It may also indicate that *the writer* knows what is going on. The pattern shows that the text has been designed. It shows that there is a design and, therefore, a designer. Furthermore, it shows that the designer is conscious of what he or she is doing. The text is not just something that tumbled unformed from the writer's mind. On the contrary, it has been shaped with a purpose.   *RG*

philosophy of composition

Your artistic manifesto. Because thinking about what you do leads to doing it better, all writers should be reflective practitioners (see **reflective writing**). A reflective practitioner will have articulated somewhere along the line a writer's manifesto, a personal philosophy of composition (the term was coined by Edgar Allan Poe). It may involve a predilection for the succinct, a preference for showing over telling, or an allergy to adverbs. Evolving your philosophy of composition will require you to look not only at your own writing but also at books on craft and theories which other practitioners have come up with – Hemingway's theory of omission, for example. A philosophy of composition ought not to be articulated once and then set in stone; it will be something that continues to evolve over time.   *RG*

phonemic patterns

A phoneme is the smallest unit of sound in the language. It is vital that a poet should pay as much attention to these minimal units of sound as they do to the whole words they make up: in a poem, the sound of the phoneme 'ar' is as important as the meaning of the word 'laugh'. Poets use similarities and differences in sound to create phonemic patterns which contribute to the overall rhythm, musicality and mood of a poem. Some of the most important phonemic patterns are **rhyme**, **alliteration**, **assonance** and consonance.   *HT*

pictures

If a picture is worth a thousand words, we're all wasting our time. However, pictures are unusually effective stimuli for writing. Finding a painting in a museum or a photograph in a book can be a wonderful starting point for a piece of work. In using pictures to write from, a helpful approach is to draw up a list of questions about the image and then jot down the answers. This will often turn out to be the raw material for some strong writing.   *RG*

plagiarism

The act of appropriating the literary composition of another author, or excerpts, ideas, or passages therefrom, and passing the material off as one's own creation – i.e. not acknowledging the source. This also applies to material on the internet; many people, mistakenly, think that because it is in the public domain this information belongs to everybody – it doesn't! This doesn't mean you can't use other people's work; just that you need to become familiar with how to acknowledge it appropriately, both within your written work and in your bibliography.

In a more diluted sense, the notion of copying another writer's style and/or ideas is something to think about. Some might say that, so long as you are getting away with it, there is nothing wrong with it. Everybody does it and there is nothing new under the sun – just make sure what you are doing is legal. If your book is similar to other successful books, the likelihood is that it will also be successful, but there is a line between knowing your market or being influenced by the canon of your genre, and stealing.   *GC*

planning

Deciding how your story may progress. The argument against planning too much is that if you know everything that's going to happen, isn't writing the novel or screenplay going to be glorified secretarial work? Many authors prefer to write to discover, which is not to say that you should sit down with a blank screen and start writing. You need some characters and a situation to get going with, but, once you have them, writing to discover is one of the joys of being a fiction writer. The opposite is studying books on plot structure and bending your characters and story into whichever ur-plot seems best to fit.   *RG*

plant and pay-off

A simple but highly effective narrative strategy where you let readers (or viewers) have a piece of information some time before they will actually need it. The plant is the first mention of the information. The pay-off comes when this information is used at a key moment in the narrative. The trick with planting is to let the reader notice but not to overemphasize the information's significance.

Rose Tremain uses plant and pay-off in three elements of the plot in her novel *The Way I Found Her*: the narrator's prowess at chess; his agility moving around on the rooftop of a Paris apartment building; and the garden hut his father is building. At several points in the novel, we are shown that Lewis, the narrator, is good at chess. The pay-off of these plants comes when winning a game of chess will be a decisive factor in whether or not he can escape from his captors at the end of the book. His skill on rooftops is also mentioned several times in the course of the book and the pay-off comes at the climax of the narrative, when he escapes his kidnappers by climbing along one roof and jumping from it to another.

Perhaps the most resonant use of plant and pay-off in *The Way I Found Her* is the way Tremain uses the garden hut that Lewis's father, Hugh, is building as a surprise for his wife when she returns from Paris. He thinks it will be nice for her to have a quiet spot in which to work. This shed crops up several times and an important aspect of the planting is that it appears that it is comic relief: because he doubts that his mother will be going back to his father, Lewis hears each report of his father's progress with a degree of contempt. We are being guided in the direction of comic relief as a distraction; while we see mentions of the garden hut in that light, we remain unaware that Tremain is busily planting. The pay-off, because we weren't expecting it, hits home with considerable resonance when it comes: it is Lewis who moves into the hut when he returns, traumatized from his ordeal. The hut turns out to be a symbolic home for Lewis. It was meant as a place of solitude for his mother, but by the conclusion of the novel, Lewis is the one who really needs the solitude.

A lovely, and, because many readers will have seen it, perhaps more easily understood example of plant and pay-off comes in the Pixar film *The Incredibles*. The costume designer Edna Mode shows Mr Incredible newsreel footage to support her view that capes aren't just unstylish on superheroes; they're dangerous. We see one caped hero after another being killed because of his cape. This newsreel footage is the plant. The pay-off comes at the climax of the film, when super-villain Syndrome is sucked into a jet engine by his cape. *RG*

play

The problem with an A to Z of Creative Writing is that it can give the impression that all you need to be a bona fide writer is to understand the facts; to know the techniques; to read the books; to talk the talk. But there's something else we all need; something so vague and nameless it doesn't fit into the alphabet, although there are a few words that stand in for it. Art is one. Play is another.

Language is not just the medium for information and narrative, it's also a kind of *stuff*, like paint or clay that can be manipulated. Babies babble. Toddlers sing nonsense songs. Schoolchildren make up codes and talk in back slang. *Ancay ouyay ememberray owhay otay peaksay itay?** Children *notice* and exploit the malleability of language but you don't have to give up word play when you become an adult. Many people do crosswords or play Scrabble but there are lots of less structured ways to play with language: jokes, puns, comic alphabets, anagrams, etc.

Play is open-ended, often using trial and error, which is good practice for creative experimentation as well as a natural way to gain confidence and control. And many fiction writers have also gone on to publish work that started off as a game. See Georges Perec's *A Void*, a novel written without the letter 'e'. Poets, particularly, need a playful eye and ear. Read Sylvia Plath's 'Metaphors', a poem in the form of a riddle with a puzzle to work out.

However, these are side effects: play doesn't necessarily get you anywhere: that's the point of it. Not everything has to have a function, a pragmatic meaning. The paradox of play is that it is both absolutely necessary and as 'useless' as clouds or roses. Ask a group of eight-year-olds to describe the useful educational qualities of hide and seek and you'll end up with a bunch of gloomy-looking kids. Loosen up. Every so often it's good to take time out from the serious but exhausting business of being a grown-up, to stop working on that weighty project every now and then and just pretend.   *HL*

(*The rules of Pig Latin or Back Slang are that you take away the first consonant and put it at the end of the word – then add *ay*. Words beginning with vowels just have *ay* at the end. So this translates as: *Can you remember how to speak it?*)

Further reading

Perec, Georges, *A Void* (London: Harvill, 1994).

plot

Events arranged to engage a reader. A plot requires **characters** and many estimable writers have suggested that plot derives from character. A corollary of this is that if an author understands his characters sufficiently, he will know what they will do in any given situation. This takes us a stage further: plot requires characters to be in a particular situation. Often this will be a situation of some **conflict**, because a plot calls for tension and tension is generated by conflict.

Characters have to react to these conflict-filled situations. They have to act and react, because stories depend on change, and if characters don't act, there can be no change. Actions, reactions and responses need to be causally linked. By now, everybody must know that the king dying followed by the queen dying is not a story but the king dying and the queen dying of heartbreak as a result is. A story is a series of causally linked events.

In a short story, sometimes the plot can be as simple as the **protagonist** or the reader realizing something. A short story may amount to no more than a situation being revealed. Novels and longer stories will need more than this, but the key to plotting a longer work of fiction may simply be deciding on a goal or ambition for the protagonist. Given such a goal, a reasonable way to construct a plot is to put obstacles in the way of this goal. Making things go wrong for your protagonist is never a bad plotting strategy.

Strong oppositions, extreme adversity, may lead to a plot reversal, which you might regard as your plot changing gear. In one of the oldest stories around, Joseph begins by having a dream in which he rules over his brothers. His first plot reversal is being sold into slavery by these same brothers. His next is being given a position of responsibility in the house of Potiphar, his new master. (Plot reversals may make things better as well as worse.) Then he ends up in jail after Potiphar's wife tries to seduce him. Eventually he is made prime minister of Egypt.

These are quite dramatic turnarounds, as plot reversals ought to be. Drama should be central to your plot. It should not be dull or too domestic; a novel about Suzy's malfunctioning washing machine will not win many readers. If a plot should not be too much like ordinary life, neither should your protagonist be too much like you or me. We may well have little experience of adultery, but *Anna Karenina* is built on it. Neither of us has been involved in murder, but the characters in both *The Lord of the Flies* and *The Secret History* have. For your plot to fly, your characters may well have to be that little bit larger than life.

These are some thoughts about plot. What about plotting, though? How is it done? In my experience, not many writers map out exactly what is going to happen in their novel before they write it. Most, to a greater or lesser extent, write to discover. They may begin by gathering thoughts about characters and situations, as Richard Ford does:

> When I start a story, while I may not have the story itself, I do have a collation of raw materials – details written in words, sentences that I've heard over time and thought were interesting, descriptions of people, memories of my own. That's the raw material for what will become the story. (Roberts et al., 2002, p. 184)

Traditionally, plots consist of beginning, middle and end. **Beginnings** are often to do with a disruption of the status quo: somebody leaves, somebody arrives, the heroine discovers she is pregnant. An inciting incident (which is after all no more than a new situation) is a means of launching a plot. The **middle** may involve reversals and the end of the middle may well be the point when all seems lost for the protagonist. Many **endings** have closure, resolving every conflict, tying up every loose end. Sometimes an ending may only contemplate a possible closure without actually letting us know whether or not it happens. With or without closure, the ending will at least signal to the reader that the story is over.

If you believe that you could benefit from a structure on which to build your plot, there are a number of books available which alert you to the archetypal nature of plots – Christopher Vogler's *The Writer's Journey*, for example – or which put forward the theory that there are only so many plots in the world and each new story is merely a recycling of one of these (Christopher Booker's *The Seven Basic Plots*, Jack M. Bickham's *20 Master Plots*).   *RG*
(See **conflict** and **narrative**)

Writing ideas

1. *Something waiting to happen*

   Sometimes a plot may be about something waiting to happen. Write a story about a married woman who circles around the possibility of a destructive affair with an unsuitable man. The story ends at the moment the affair begins.

2. *Character and situation*

   Write down one- or two-word summaries of a number of characters (loser; postman; flirt; egomaniac, etc). Next write down an equal number of potentially dramatic situations (stuck in a train carriage with someone who likes to bore on; in a boundary dispute with a neighbour; late at night in the city after losing wallet or purse; crashing a borrowed car, etc). Cut out individually all the characters and all the situations, crumple up the pieces of paper and put all the character descriptions in one mug and all the situation descriptions in another mug. Now pick one from each mug, put them together and start writing.

Further reading

Lamott, Anne, *Bird By Bird – Some Instructions on Writing and Life* (New York: Anchor Books, 1995).

Roberts, James, Barry Mitchell and Roger Zubrinich (eds), *Writers on Writing* (Victoria: Penguin Books Australia, 2002).

poetic genres

Traditional poetic genres are derived from the ancient Greek genres, the **lyric**, the **epic** and the **drama**, which together form the origins of Western writing. The lyric gave birth to the short poem. The Greek epic was a long narrative poem, usually focused on the history of the people, rather than personal feelings. The natural descendant of the epic is the **novel**, but poetic epics are still produced today. The storytelling impulse in poetry moved into the **ballad** in the late middle ages. Greek drama was the originator of theatrical writing, but also of verse drama and poetic **monologue**. The latter has had a revival in recent years in the writing of Carol Ann Duffy and Paul Durcan. Try writing in another person's voice as an exercise in working with language, tone and narrative in poetry.

In addition to the major genres, there are numerous sub-genres, often written for particular occasions or in a particular mood. These too have their contemporary descendants and you are likely to have read or even written at least one of the following:

- elegies, commemorating a person's death;
- epithalamiums, celebrating a wedding;
- pastoral poems, celebrating natural life, particularly in contrast to the urban;
- satires, mocking an individual or an institution (at the heart of much political poetry);
- parodies, sending up other poems, literary works or even advertising;
- religious poems, such as hymns and psalms;
- odes, in praise of a person, abstract value or object.

While some of these ancient poetic genres have complex formal structures, which are not usually followed today, they engage with life in ways that remain central to poetry now as then.   *HT*

poetry

What exactly is poetry? We all think we know but very few people, including most poets, can agree on an absolute definition. 'A poem', wrote the American poet, Sylvia Plath, is 'concentrated, a closed fist'. Poems do tend to appear in shorter form than the other major genres. Even longer works, many would argue, use language in the intense, evocative way that Plath implies. 'Poetic language' is more likely to be symbolic, rather than narrative, either because it uses recognizable **imagery** or because it invites the reader to see events and objects as representative rather than realistic. This means that there are many ways to read a poem; poems engage in multiple, rather than closed, meanings. As such, poetry demands a good deal from its readers, but also gives them greater freedom to join in with the creative endeavour. Every true reader of poetry is also a writer, in that they enjoy working creatively with language in order to find and create meanings. This element of poetry, its challenge to the reader, also means that it is sometimes regarded as difficult or elitist, evoking fear even in the most confident prose or script writer who has strayed into a general creative writing class and is required to produce a token poem or two.

If you are fearful of poetry, it is worth remembering that poetry is not just about trying to create or crack a code; it is also about working with the sound of language. The Northumbrian modernist poet, Basil Bunting, expressed this simply: 'Poetry deals in sounds – long sounds and short sounds, heavy beats and light beats, the tone relations of vowels, the relations of consonants to one another which are like instrumental colour in music.' If writers and readers of poetry were to accept its musicality more wholeheartedly, there would be less agonizing over meanings and metaphors and more pleasure taken in the rhythms of language.

How do you achieve this musical relationship to language? You need to read widely and to read aloud. Anthologies and websites are the best (and cheapest) places to begin but you could also attend **poetry readings and performances** by established writers, working towards giving these yourself. This process of reading and listening, writing and performing, will help you to find your own 'poetic voice'.

The next essential skill is editing, drafting and redrafting your work. This can be a lonely business, so make use of any local writers' groups, classes or friends who will give you honest feedback. Finally, the devices described elsewhere in the poetry entries within this book are key. The poet must work with **metre** and/or **rhythm**, with structure and form (see **lineation**) and with the sonic quality of the words themselves through patterns of recurrence (see **phonemic patterns** and **repetition**). This is how poetry is made.

These techniques comprise what is often called 'the poetic craft'. Poets can and do argue to the point of weariness over the relationship of form to content but, fundamentally, most would agree that poetry 'is not made with ideas, it is made with words'. This succinct formulation originates from the early-twentieth-century French poet Mallarmé (arguably, the inventor of free verse). The poetic craft is then central to any definition of poetry, whether it be the mastery of **fixed forms**, such as the villanelle, or the individualistic, intensely worked, structures of **experimental poetry**.

This does not mean that the subject matter of poetry is of no significance. Its raw material, as with any writing, is life, and there are some key threads in the poetic approach to life. In many poems of all types, we find close obser-vation and tiny details which may be the minutiae of natural or urban life, the body of a lover, social interactions or language itself. The poem focuses our attention on these details and invites us to see them as significant, leaping between the micro and the macro, drawing the reader into the realm of the metaphysical.

We are now entering the second century to be dominated by free verse (that is poetry which does not conform to a set **metre** or rhyme scheme) and it becomes more and more difficult to define poetry by specific formal devices. We'd be surprised these days to hear a poem described as a 'momentary stay against confusion', as Robert Frost claimed. At its wilder edges, poetry now appears in increasingly chaotic and diverse forms, visually and sonically, and uses language in every possible register and structure. In the light of all of that, do any of our definitions stand and does it really matter how we define poetry? Only you, from your reading and your writing, can decide.   *HT*

Writing ideas

Inside/outside exercise

- Step outside into the wider world (anywhere from a shopping street to a woodland).
- Choose three small visual details that interest you.
- Divide your page into two columns, 'outside' and 'inside'.
- Write a description of the three micro details in your 'outside' column and write what they make you think or feel in your inside column.
- Weaving between the two columns of text, can you select words and images to make a poem?   *HT*

Further reading

Herbert, W. N. and Matthew Hollis (eds), *Strong Words: Modern Poets on Modern Poetry* (Northumberland: Bloodaxe Books, 2000). The quotations cited above all come from this volume.

Rothenberg, Jerome, *Poems for the Millennium: the University of California Book of Modern and Postmodern Poetry* (2 vols) (Berkeley: University of California Press, 1995 and 1998).

Sweeney, Matthew and J. H. Williams, *Writing Poetry: and Getting Published* (London: Hodder Headline, 1997).

Timpane, John and Maureen Watts, *Poetry for Dummies* (New York: For Dummies, 2001).

poetry readings and performances

Poetry has been performed throughout history and only in performance can its sonic and musical qualities be fully appreciated. Contemporary poetry readings are usually simple affairs, with one or two poets reading for 20 to 40 minutes from their current work. Performance poetry refers to work with strong storytelling, experimental, political or personal aspects leading to a more dramatic performance, sometimes using music or physical props. Performances take place in arts centres, bookshops, pubs, libraries, church halls, schools, colleges, libraries and theatres.

Poetry slams and open-mike nights are becoming increasingly popular for lesser-known and student poets. If you are starting out in poetry, testing your work on an audience, hearing it aloud in a public setting will help you edit and refine it. These events are usually open to all comers and have an energetic, sometimes raucous, atmosphere. The poetry slam is competitive, judged either by the audience or by a panel of judges. Competitors are given about three minutes to impress, which requires quick-fire and accessible work. Be prepared. Poetry events usually involve a drink before, during or after, sometimes all three. Booze may relax the audience and alleviate the sometimes stilted atmosphere of a reading, but it does nothing for your carefully rehearsed set if the words are leaping manically about the page.

How do you prepare for a reading? Attend other readings and gain experience of the worst and the best of poetry performance. Practice reading your own work, focusing on pace, pitch and projection. This is the only way to overcome nerves and create a strong set. Choose your poems carefully, thinking of variety in length and tone. Work out how much talking you want to do: it is important to appear human to your audience but vital not to be a rambling bore. Have the confidence to let the work speak for itself. Be true to the poem on the page, pacing according to your own line-breaks, spacing and structure, and bringing out the rhythm of the piece. Body language can help here: try to inhabit the space confidently, looking up and incorporating some movement or hand gestures into your performance.

Whatever sort of poetry you write, the best way to start performing is with a small circle of friends, fellow poets or students. In that context, you can build up confidence and receive honest feedback in order to help you work towards the more public forms of performance. Why not set up a poetry group in your home or university and see where it takes you?   *HT*

Further reading and listening
Poetry Slam, www.poetryslam.com.
Robinson, Mark, *Words Out Loud: ten essays about poetry readings* (Exeter: Stride, 2002).
Write Out Loud, www.writeoutloud.net.

point of view

The vantage point, to use Janet Burroway's term, from which we experience the story. This vantage point is situated close to or within the viewpoint character, which is to say the person from whose perspective we access the story.

A crucial narrative choice – perhaps the earliest one – is deciding from whose point of view the fiction should be written. This may be the protagonist or it may be another character who is able closely to observe the protagonist. Once you have made your mind up about which of the available characters will narrate your story, the next decision facing you is the form this narrator will take. There are a few options.

Omniscient narration, which is where the narrator speaks as though he or she were God, was used liberally in the nineteenth century. In contemporary practice, authors either deploy the omniscient sparingly, or avoid advertising the fact that they are using this form. Or if they are using it broadly, they may adopt an ironic tone to show that they know that excessive use of omniscience is old-fashioned.

First person ('I') makes it possible for your narrator to appear to have an intimate relationship with the reader. First person allows the reader to know more about the inner world of the narrator, to address readers directly, to confide in them. There are also shortcomings, the most obvious of which is that a first person narrator has to be present whenever anything important happens. In addition, it's all too easy in first person to grow so introspective that the plot is neglected.

Third person point of view ('she' or 'he') is as common as first person and has the same virtues, but with the added advantage that the perspective, the vantage point, may be adjusted. Third person may be subjective or objective – in other words, the author may inhabit the consciousness of the character or remain on the surface of that character so that readers have access to the narrator's thoughts and feelings, or not. The following, from Sebastian Faulks' *Birdsong*, is an example of the former:

> She looked into the staring face of her father, the eyes dark and remote above the thick moustache. How hard he would find it to understand what she was doing, she thought. How little he had ever tried. (Faulks, 1994, p. 80)

In this passage, though, Cormac McCarthy remains on the surface of his viewpoint character:

> He looked at the phone lying there on the table. He picked it up and pulled the cord out of it and put it back in the cradle. Then he went over and stood at the door, his thumb on the hammer of the shotgun. (McCarthy, 2005, p. 110)

Third person narration also offers you the option of adjusting the focus which first person does not. This adjusting of the focus is what John Gardner talks of when he uses the term 'psychic distance', which he defines as 'the distance the reader feels between himself and the events in the story' (Gardner, 1991, p. 111). Look at this passage from Raymond Carver's story 'They're Not Your Husband':

> Earl Ober was between jobs as a salesman. But Doreen, his wife, had gone to work nights as a waitress at a twenty-four-hour coffee shop on the edge of town. One night, when he was drinking, Earl decided to stop by the coffee shop and have something to eat. He wanted to see where Doreen worked and he wanted to see if he could order something on the house . . .
> He sat at the counter and studied the menu. (Carver, 1989, p. 44)

The first paragraph is omniscient narration, but as soon as the second paragraph begins, it becomes third person: the viewpoint is Earl's; we have entered the moment he is in. Here you see the versatility of third person. It allows the author to move the vantage point from somewhere up in the sky with the godlike narrator to right inside a viewpoint character. Gardner's psychic distance goes from immense to minute. Not possible in first person narration.

A further viewpoint option is second person:

> How did you get here? It was your friend, Tad Allagash, who powered you in here, and he has disappeared. Tad is the kind of guy who would be at a place like this at this time of the morning. He is either your best self or your worst self, you're not sure which. (McInerney, 1986, p. 2)

Like first person, this has the advantage of intimacy with the reader; here the author effects to make reader and viewpoint character one. However, it's rare enough to still appear an affectation.

It's possible to control the distance between the reader and the events of the story not just by adjusting the position of your vantage point but also by adjusting the position of the narrator in relation to the events of the story and to the reader. The point of view character may be within the action, as Delores, Trezza Azzopardi's narrator in *The Hiding Place*, is here:

> I put my lolly in my mouth so that I can lift the sewing-box off the sideboard. It's been pushed to the back, it's a bit of a stretch and before I can grasp it, the box slides off and upends itself on the mat. Everything spills out. (Azzopardi, 2000, p. 134)

But here, at another point in the same novel, is Dolores addressing the reader directly:

> This is my bedroom, and Luca's, and Fran's, and my mother's. The four of us sleep here, and at the back of the house live Celesta and Rose, my other two sisters who I don't really know. (*ibid.*, p. 4)

Whichever of the above viewpoints you choose, a further source of variety is to write a dual viewpoint narrative. Here the vantage point alternates between two characters. This allows for two conflicting views of the same events. Also, each time you move from one viewpoint character to another, you introduce change, and change in a narrative is always healthy, always likely to increase reader engagement. From dual, it's a natural progression to multiple viewpoint, which offers writer and reader the chance to move around between a handful of viewpoint characters. *No Country For Old Men* is a multiple viewpoint novel, but this example from it shows how a shift may be made between two viewpoint characters. We begin in the viewpoint of the hero, Sheriff Bell, and then move into that of the villain:

> I ain't sure we've seen these people before. Their kind. I don't know what to do about em even. If you killed em all they'd have to build a annex on to hell.
>
> Chigurh pulled in to the Desert Aire shortly before noon and parked just below Moss's trailer and shut off the engine. He got out and walked across the raw dirt yard and climbed the steps and tapped at the aluminium door. (McCarthy, 2005, p. 79)

In the handling of viewpoint, the crucial factor is consistency. One of the most glaring errors a learning writer may make is the viewpoint lapse. For instance, the author is for most of the story in a particular viewpoint, but at one stage accidentally slips into the perspective of another character, perhaps by recording the thoughts of a non-viewpoint character. Such lapses undermine the reader's suspension of disbelief; the credibility of your fiction is destroyed in a second.   *RG*

Writing ideas

1. *Adjusting viewpoint*

   A woman is walking with her dog on a beach. She passes a pub and, up ahead, can see the ruins of a castle. Then she meets someone she knows. Begin in omniscient and, when it feels right, move into the woman's viewpoint, in limited third person point of view.

2. *Psychic distance*

   Your narrator is in the present (Point 2 in space or time). The story happened five years ago (Point 1 in space or time). The reader represents Point 3 in space or time. Write two pages of fiction in which you adjust the distance between these three points several times. Your stimulus: a conflict between employee and manager.

3. *Dual viewpoint*

   Using dual viewpoint, write a 1,500-word short story about the beginnings of a romantic relationship.

Further reading

Azzopardi, Trezza, *The Hiding Place* (London: Picador, 2000).

Burroway, Janet, *Writing Fiction: A Guide To Narrative Craft*, sixth edition (New York: Longman, 2003).

Carver, Raymond, *Where I'm Calling From* (New York: Vintage, 1989).

Faulks, Sebastian, *Birdsong* (London: Vintage, 1994).

Gardner, John, *The Art of Fiction: Notes on Craft for Young Writers* (New York: Vintage, 1991).

McCarthy, Cormac, *No Country For Old Men* (London: Picador, 2005).

McInerney, Jay, *Bright Lights, Big City* (London: Flamingo, 1986).

political correctness

The much-ridiculed idea that we should be careful of the language that we use to avoid offence to disadvantaged groups. There are many apocryphal (mainly false) stories of loony-left councils imposing silly politically correct (PC) rules on the public. True or not, any attempt to control language, however well-meaning, is particularly challenging for writers. The bottom line is that we can and should write what we like: the mind is a private space and the writer should be free to tell the truth as they see it. Many books now recognized as innovative and truthful have initially been denigrated or banned. Others, once seen as acceptable, are now recognized as oppressive. However, society is made up of many competing voices and any intervention, of which writing is one, involves a balance between honesty, personal freedom and the rights and freedoms of others.   *HL*

(See **thought police**)

postmodernism

A disputed and complex term, which, like **modernism**, refers to a historical period (the second half of the twentieth century), a cultural movement and a set of ideas. As some people have commented, the twenty-first century is in the post-postmodern period. And as other people have commented, 'Stop it! Now!' The term *postmodernist* has become an over-used generalization as well as a bit of a joke, but there are many useful insights and ideas which find their way into contemporary fiction and poetry. These include multiple narratives, as in Paul Auster's *New York Trilogy*, and the undermining of fixed divisions between genres and forms, as seen in W. G. Sebald's and Jeanette Winterson's work. Another key aspect of postmodernism is the questioning of the hierarchy between popular and literary writing, and of the relationship between representation and the thing represented, as in Borges' *Fictions*. There is also the insight that readers create their own meaning as you are doing in this very po-mo moment.   *HL*

(See **Death of the Author; metafiction**)

premise

The premise is the question that the story is going to answer. If the question was 'What if toys suffered from jealousy?' the answer might be the *Toy Story* screenplay. If it was 'What would happen if a nice guy ended up inheriting the role of mafia boss?' the answer might be *The Godfather*. Checking to see if what you write addresses the premise's question is a useful way of seeing what does and doesn't belong in the story. The premise of a story has also been called the promise of what it will be about.   *RG*

proofreading

The process of making sure your typescript is up to standard. There is absolutely no excuse for poor presentation, bad spelling or poor grammar. If the writer cannot be bothered to ensure that the typescript is word-perfect, why should an agent or an editor be bothered to read it? Proofreading is a laborious but essential part of the redrafting process and is often eased by grammar and spelling checks on your word-processing software. Make sure that the program is correct for your market. Useful techniques include asking a friend or colleague to read the script. They are more likely to spot your own habitual errors or personal quirks. You can also read the piece aloud, or, better still, record it and play it back. A good idea is to leave the script alone for a week or even a month before proofreading, thus distancing yourself from your work. On a more creative level, proofreading is crucial for ensuring continuity of plotting and timelines, and also consistency of character traits.   *GC*

prose

A first response might be that prose is writing which isn't poetry. But is a screenplay prose? Prose is the form of language in which the vast majority of written communication, from newspaper stories to a masterpiece like *Crime and Punishment*, comes. Traditionally, prose is thought to be less artful, less constructed and structured, than poetry, but, as books like this one strive to make clear, all writing should have all three of those virtues.   *RG*

prose poetry

Short pieces of writing, set out on the page as prose but using poetic devices, such as **rhythm**, **repetition** and **imagery**, and so recognizable as poetry, despite abandoning the line-break. See Gertrude Stein's *Tender Buttons*, written in 1914, and Robert Sheppard, writing today.   *HT*

Further reading

Sheppard, Robert, 'Histories of Sensation' and 'Internal Exile' in *The Flashlight Sonata* (Exeter: Stride, 1993).

Stein, Gertrude, *Tender Buttons* (Mineola, NY: Dover Publications, 1988).

protagonist

The central figure, main character or hero(ine) of a narrative. The person, if you like, whose story this is. In fiction, the protagonist may or may not be the **point of view** character. Protagonists will usually have a wish or a goal and a narrative is created as they overcome the impediments to this goal (see **simple linear plot**). In struggling to overcome these impediments, the protagonist should demonstrate determination and courage. In dramatic fiction and Hollywood screenplays, protagonists ought to be bigger than ordinary mortals – stronger, faster, braver, less vulnerable. Overcoming all opposition on the way to their goal ought to change the protagonist. And opposition, obviously, will often come in human form – the antagonist. In *Chinatown*, it's Noah Cross; in *One Flew Over The Cuckoo's Nest*, it's Nurse Ratchett.   *RG*

publishing

The process which takes a script to the shelf. Happy with your script, your agent will discuss with you the options for selling the book and this is usually done by approaches to a selected few publishers or a blanket sending of the book to all likely publishers with a date for final responses (an auction). The latter is clearly a higher-risk strategy because if nobody bites, the book has absolutely nowhere to go. Your bridges are burned. With the former approach, you and your agent, in the event of wholesale rejection, can take on board the reasons for decline and absorb the comments into a further redraft before going out to other publishers.

Once you or your agent has had a script accepted by an editor at a publishing house, you will negotiate and agree basic terms. Issues which will be raised are: the amount and timings of the advance; the royalty rate for hardback, paperback and any international rights; the publication date (for hardback and paperback); the marketing budget; and the publisher's strategy for raising your profile.

Even though your editor has championed and bought your book, they will almost certainly require you to undertake a redraft and you will probably receive a detailed list of changes which they want you to consider and implement. Once this redraft has been done, the manuscript will be sent to a copy-editor for more precision editing. After this, a proof copy will be produced and jacket design, author photograph, biography, acknowledgements and dedications will be agreed. You will be assigned a publicity officer to place features, articles, get reviews, arrange personal appearances, readings, signings and TV/radio interviews, and you will also draw up a list of people to whom proof copies will be sent for review or comments for the jacket.

Once the hardback is launched, much of the book's success will depend on the publisher's sales team, whose job it is to visit the booksellers and negotiate orders. The more copies the booksellers order, the more prominence the book will gain within the shops. A major bonus at this stage is if the sales force can negotiate for your book to be included in store special offers, such as '3 for the price of 2'. The same process is repeated for the paperback launch, but in greater numbers and with the benefit of the reviews received for the hardback.

There are a myriad of publishers and these are listed in the writers' handbooks. However, there are fewer publishers than most people think. A single publisher is likely to have more than one imprint (a market-related brand which represents a list of titles occupying a similar appeal to a specific readership). Your editor will probably represent only one imprint within the publishing house, but will most likely have worked for different imprints at different stages of their career.

As an example, Transworld has several imprints, namely: Doubleday, Black Swan, Bantam and Corgi. You may be familiar with these imprints but, as an example, Black Swan publishes Kate Atkinson, Bantam publishes Danielle Steel, and Corgi publishes Catherine Cookson. To complicate matters, in 2001 Transworld merged with Random House (whose imprints include Cape, Secker and Warburg, Chatto and Windus, William Heinemann, Century, Hutchinson, and Arrow). And as if the machine isn't big enough, Transworld is ultimately owned by the Bertelsmann Group, a media and entertainment conglomerate which rivals Disney and Warner Brothers in size and market dominance. Your book is likely to be a small cog in an extremely large machine. That is not to say that your relationship with your editor and publicist will not be intimate. Also, there are many smaller and independent publishers who operate outside the domain of the major players, such as Bloodaxe and Tindall Street Press. It may be difficult to imagine but Liz Calder set up Bloomsbury a few decades ago as a small independent press and now they sell millions upon millions of copies of *Harry Potter*. The important thing is to get to know your publishers and their imprints. Become familiar with their catalogues and who they publish. Research deeper into who is publishing what and how they relate to the types of books you are writing. Know your market by visiting bookshops and reading, reading, reading. GC

Further reading
Turner, Barry (ed.), *The Writer's Handbook* (London: Pan, published annually).
The Writers' and Artists' Yearbook (London: A & C Black, also published annually).
And, if you can find a copy:
Gordon, Giles, *Aren't We Due a Royalty Statement?: A Stern Account of Literary, Publishing and Theatrical Folk* (London: Chatto and Windus, 1993).

punctuation

Lynne Truss defines punctuation as both traffic signals telling us to slow down, detour or stop and, quoting a newspaper style-book, as 'a courtesy designed to help readers to understand a story without stumbling'. Like grammatical errors (see **grammar**), incorrect punctuation only signals to your readers that you don't know what you're doing.

Here's a quick guide to things that commonly go wrong in punctuation. Make sure your sentences really are sentences. Note the difference between a colon and a semicolon: the former goes before a list or an example, while the latter breaks a sentence in two, usually into a main clause followed by a modifier. Punctuation of direct speech always goes inside the speech marks. Questions always need a question mark.   RG

(See also **apostrophes**)

quest plot

The quest plot is fuelled by desire: its protagonist searches for a person, place or thing she believes will change her life. For examples, you can plunder fairy tales, epics and myths from all over the world. Their structures have withstood the test of time, and their inherent mystery means that though they can be updated, they can never be over-written. Patricia Duncker, for instance, looks back to Homer for a basic narrative pattern that has delighted listeners and readers for two millennia.

The *Odyssey*, says Duncker, is the prototype of the quest plot: tired of wandering, Odysseus wants to go home. Famous examples of quest plots include Thomas Malory's *Le Morte d'Arthur* (the knights search for the Holy Grail); Charlotte Brontë's *Jane Eyre* (Jane wishes to find her true home); Joseph Conrad's *Lord Jim* (Jim searches for his lost honour); coming-of-age stories (or *bildungsromans*) such as J. D. Salinger's *The Catcher in the Rye* (the protagonist wants to grow up); coming-out stories such as Edmund White's *A Boy's Own Story*; cowboy stories; and revenge plots.

In the quest plot your characters can take to the road and your cast can grow or shrink. The danger is that you can lose focus and confuse your reader, so devise a strong protagonist to hold your story together. Though Steven Spielberg's *Indiana Jones and the Last Crusade* has the Holy Grail as the object of the hunt, the search, as Ronald B. Tobias points out, has no effect on the hero as a human being. Thus the plot is an adventure rather than a quest. The ending of the quest can be either ecstatic or tragic, or somewhere in between. But the protagonist must have been altered by the process.

The complement of the quest plot is the siege plot, in which characters are trapped physically, emotionally or psychologically. Stories of literal sieges include Homer's *Iliad* (about the siege of Troy), Albert Camus's *The Plague* (characters are marooned in a town during an epidemic) and Ann Patchett's *Bel Canto* (an opera cast is besieged by terrorists). Emotional or psychological sieges include family dramas such as Ivy Compton-Burnett's *A House and Its*

Head, love stories such as L. P. Hartley's *The Go-Between*, detective stories, country house murder plots, and war stories.

Siege plots work best with a limited cast and not too many subplots. As Duncker points out, because they depend on steadily mounting tension, the main risk is that your writing can turn flat. Implant **conflict** at every stage, and make sure that your high points are triggered by your **protagonist**. Otherwise, he or she may distance your reader by seeming unlikeably passive. If you fear the pace of your novel is flagging, put a clock on the story.

As in Henry James's *The Portrait of a Lady*, quest plots easily turn into siege plots (and even back again), showing that these two patterns are interlinked. Whichever you choose, remember that talented plotting depends less on whodunnit than on *why* they did it.   *JN*

quilting

Stitching together sections or chapters which, when completed, form a picture. In this patchwork of text, each patch will contrast with its neighbours in a similar way to what you might find on a patchwork quilt. The contrast might be that two neighbouring scraps of text are in different viewpoints or set in a different place or time. Amy Tan's *The Joy Luck Club* is an example of this kind of quilting. It has eight viewpoint characters and is set in 1980s America and in China earlier in the twentieth century. The contrast between the scraps of text might be the use of different narrative strategies. One text might be standard fictional discourse consisting of **narrative** passage and **dialogue**, while next to it another text might have the appearance of a press interview. You can find these two approaches juxtaposed in David Mitchell's novel *Cloud Atlas*. The insertion of letters – the **epistolary** – in conventional fictional discourse is another approach to quilting.

Elaine Showalter examines narrative quilting in her critical work *Sister's Choice*, in which she argues that nineteenth-century American women writers were freed from the pressures of the novel form by, as Showalter puts it, 'working with the piece or the story'. In her account of this development, women writers, because of domestic responsibilities and the difficulties of being financially independent, were attracted to the greater freedom that the short-story form – 'the short narrative piece' – permitted. The increasing status of the novel in America caused them to collect their stories together, and, in some cases, evolve them into novels 'with narrative structures developed out of the piecing technique' (Showalter, 1991, p. 158). In other words, the patchwork quilt inspired these narrative structures.

To illustrate how women writers in America at this time developed this approach to narrative, Showalter examines Kate Chopin's short story 'Elizabeth Stock's Story'. The eponymous protagonist wants to write, but is put off by masculine narrative forms she describes as 'original, entertaining, full of action, and goodness knows what all'. Instead, she produces writing made up of patches of narrative in the same way quilts may be made up of scraps of fabric. Elizabeth Stock dies and her work is collected and shaped by a male editor, who imposes an order on it, putting together some pages which 'bore any semblance to a connected or consecutive narration' (Chopin, 1983, p. 274).

In contemporary examples of the quilted narrative, order is suggested by a conclusion which draws together some of the threads of the various patches of narrative, or which suggests closure. Both are evident in the conclusions to *The Joy Luck Club* and Carol Shields' *Larry's Party*. At the end of the former, the central conflict of the novel, the tension the daughters of the book feel between being Chinese and American, is resolved, when one of them goes to China to come to terms with the Chinese part of her identity. In *Larry's Party*, the final chapter is a dinner party which unites the major characters of the novel and thus offers some sort of closure for Larry.

The quilted narrative can offer an escape from more plot-driven forms and a greater variety of narrative strategy. At the same time, it's possible to pull things together at the conclusion in a way that gives the quilted form the appearance of its more conventional relative.   *RG*

Further reading

Chopin, Kate, *The Awakening And Selected Stories* (London and New York: Penguin, 1983), p. 274.

Mitchell, David, *Cloud Atlas* (London: Sceptre, 2005).

Shields, Carol, *Larry's Party* (London: Fourth Estate, 1998).

Showalter, Elaine, *Sister's Choice: Tradition and Change in American Women's Writing* (New York: Clarendon Press, 1991).

Tan, Amy, *The Joy Luck Club* (London: Vinatge, 1991).

race

The simple dictionary definitions of race refer to the divisions between human groups and to ethnic origin. However, the term also has powerful cultural and value-laden connotations and its use as a 'scientific' term of classification is now seen by most as politically suspect. As with any volatile issue, the language of ethnic difference changes rapidly, often leaving speakers and writers of all kinds and origins uncertain, intimidated and wordless.

There are a number of aspects to race and ethnicity for writers to consider. One is the recognition that we live in a multi-ethnic society, and although we are certainly not *required* to produce didactic or **politically correct** work, neither can we ignore the complex world we live in. Another issue is that black and Asian writers may need to resist being stereotyped as primarily concerned with race issues. Mike Phillips, a UK crime writer originally from Guyana, argues that some black writers have tended to become imprisoned 'within the idea of race and blackness' and that he deliberately chose the crime genre in order to challenge that expectation (Procter, 2002).

Another factor is discrimination: some argue that black and Asian writers have greater difficulty in getting published than white writers, and a report published by *The Bookseller* and the UK Arts Council in 2006 found that although 7.9 per cent of the UK population is of ethnic minority origin, only 1 per cent of the year's bestsellers were by black and ethnic minority writers.

On the other hand, there are many success stories. In the UK, Monica Ali, Malorie Blackman, Hari Kunzru, Andrea Levy, Zadie Smith, Benjamin Zephaniah, for example, have all become widely read and recognized. In the United States, Toni Morrison, Alex Haley, Alice Walker and Maya Angelou, among a great many others, have won national and international recognition. These exceptional writers should help to inspire confidence and ambition in others.   *HL*

Further reading

African American Literature: http://en.wikipedia.org/wiki/African_American_literature.

radio

The Arts Council: www.artscouncil.org.uk.

Contemporary Writers: www.contemporarywriters.com.

Procter, James, 'Mike Phillips' (2002) on *Contemporary Writers*, www.contemporary writers.com/authors/?p=auth208.

radio

Writing for radio is all about sound: the listener only knows what is going on through the ear. As Gill Adams, radio scriptwriter, says, 'Radio can be as wild as your imagination will allow – you can go to the moon or be inside a womb – it's as visual as film and as intimate as a novel.' There are many opportunities for writers on radio. The BBC, for example, has a number of short-story and drama slots, regularly calling for script submissions, and offering support and advice for writers of all kind. There are also a number of independent companies, agents and producers who commission scripts and stories for radio.

Many of our best playwrights first honed their skills in radio. BBC Radio 4 broadcasts an afternoon play every day, and a play each Friday evening. Radio 3 offers *The Wire* for experimental radio drama, *Drama on 3*, and *The Verb*, a showcase for new writing and performance. Both Radio 3 and Radio 4 offer the Listen Again facility via the bbc.co.uk radio web pages, so you can hear programmes at your own convenience. Click on the Speech and Drama web pages on the Radio 3 home site, www.bbc.co.uk/radio3, or the Arts and Drama web pages on the Radio 4 home site, www.bbc.co.uk/radio4.   *HL and HN*

Further reading

BBC Writers' Room: www.bbc.co.uk/writersroom.

The Independent Radio Drama Production website: www.irdp.co.uk.

Writer's Net: www.writernet.co.uk.

reader(s)

People who read your work. You want to attract them, engage them, involve their emotions and leave them feeling fulfilled, sated and, with luck, changed. When you write, you consciously or unconsciously have in mind an ideal reader, who is probably someone like yourself. 'The ideal reader of my novels', Anthony Burgess said, 'is a lapsed Catholic and failed musician, short sighted, colour-blind, auditorially biased, who has read the books that I have read. He should also be about my age.' (Plimpton, 1992, p. 94)   *RG*

reading

The place of reading is not the book but the mind, an infinite space in which we make up the world and ourselves. Reading is where writing begins. Joanne Harris, author of *Chocolat,* says that she started writing as a child because she didn't want the story to end. Reading and writing are the two-in-one sides of the Möbius strip: a continuum. Reading is the essential engine, the creative source, almost as necessary to the writer as air.

By the time we are ten or eleven, we have forgotten those eureka moments we used to have, when the meaning suddenly emerged out of incomprehension, and we found ourselves actually reading. In skilled readers this process is fast and seamless: words on the page become image, voice, action – the reader slips through the words like Alice through the looking glass into the story world on the other side. Francis Spufford describes his first experience of this:

> I was six with the yellow hardback copy of *The Hobbit* in my hands; and the pictures came. I went to the door of the hobbit hole with Bilbo . . . I jogged along with him on his pony out of the Shire. (Spufford, 2000, p. 69)

For writers, as for everybody else, the first and most important thing is to read for pleasure. Find the writers you like and read as much of their work as you can. Be wide-ranging and adventurous. Choose books because you like the sound of the title or the picture on the book cover. Read love stories, science fiction, horror, magic, rap poetry, nineteenth-century novels, chick-lit. Read until you've had enough, read until you're sick. If you're not sure what to read, browse the library shelves and skim the first paragraph of half a dozen books until something hooks you in. Read the reviews in broadsheet newspapers. Ask a bookworm friend to make recommendations. There is a big world of books out there and in order to develop your own writing voice you need to have read a wide range of other voices. The point is to become addicted to *reading itself.*

There are times and circumstances where you just want to read something easy and relaxing: holiday reading, one of those stories that slip down like strawberry ice cream or strong lager. But at other times we need to push beyond the limits of habit and safety, to read with more attention and effort. If you are not already an experienced and confident reader, then this will be hard at first. You will try things that don't immediately appeal; you will struggle with unfamiliar ideas, strange voices. You may feel awkward and wrong-footed, floundering in what feels like an alien language, deliberately designed to confuse and exclude you. This is painful and you might be tempted to give up, to blame the writing or the writer: *it's rubbish, incomprehensible, pretentious, deliberately obscure.* Remember that reading is a process of self-development, of learning and changing. If *everything* you read is easy, accessible, straightforward and familiar, you're not doing it right. You don't have to *like* everything you read but it sometimes pays not to give up too soon: some exceptional pleasures take time to understand, to learn to like.

After reading for pleasure comes reading as a writer: reading to find out *how it was done.* This is not the same as critical reading by a literature tutor or student in an English class. The critical reader looks at the piece of writing *as a whole*: an existing artefact in the world, a solid *thing*, almost as natural as rock. What matters to the critic is making meaning and contextualization out of this object. The *process* of writing itself, the *work* of the writer is largely unexplored in conventional literary studies.

Writers need to develop a double vision: to read like normal people – following the story as a continuous drama. But they also need to look beneath the surface of the print for traces of *the making process*, the writer at work. We need to deconstruct the work's structures, shapes and forms: to see how it *works*.

There are many ways you can do this and there is no absolutely right way. For example, you could take two pages of any piece of writing and remember that once it was nothing at all, not even a thought. Imagine those very first notes: one or two words scribbled on a scrap of paper; two or three ideas still unconnected; a voice whispering in the writer's ear; a door, a face. Beneath the surface of this polished piece of work in front of you is a first draft: messy, muddled, vague and unformed. Just like most first drafts – like yours and mine.

A word of warning: we can never *completely* understand a piece of writing; there will always be some parts that are beyond deconstruction. Writing is not rocket science; it's much more complex than that. Fiction, poetry, etc. is made out of the writer's consciousness interacting with culture, time and place. And when we bring *our* consciousness, as readers, to bear, we begin to change a piece of writing simply by reading it. Any creative process involves intuition, emotion, play, all of which, by their nature, are beyond final and complete analysis. However, there is much we *can* learn that is useful: skills and processes, techniques, methods, *know-how.*   *HL*

Further reading
Manguel, Alberto, *A History of Reading* (London: Flamingo, 1997).
Spufford, Francis, *The Child That Books Built* (London: Faber, 2000).

reading as a writer

Take any piece of writing. Look at the first line. Does it hook or repel you? This may be the only thing a prospective reader will read before they put the book down or take it to the cash till. It should make you want to read on. Read the first paragraph. Does the writing move along with an obvious narrative line or does it jump from one voice, idea or description to another? Is this writing that carries you along with it like a boat on a river or is it more like a puzzle, a maze?

As you read, also look at the way the writing is made. Tease out the different elements: **character**, **setting**, **pace**, **plot**. Dig down deep into the *stuff* of the writing: read its entrails, find its buried codes; look back through the mirror of words until you can almost see the writer behind it, at work. *HL*

realism

When you write realist fiction you describe the world as you see, understand and hear it, or believe that it used to be, and not as it might, or ought, to be. Your characters will, loosely speaking, 'live' in your readers' minds; and however contrived your plot, you will seek to make it seem possible if not probable. Realist writers aim to wrap their readers in what American novelist and critic John Gardner describes as 'the fictional dream': the illusion that, while they are reading a novel, they inhabit a realm as solid as their own, everyday world, and subject to similar laws.

Realist tenets were challenged by so-called experimental twentieth-century movements such as modernism and postmodernism, both of which questioned the notion of a 'reality' shared between author and reader. But no novelist has ever tried to hold what Hamlet describes as 'a mirror up to nature'. As we shall see below, far from merely reflecting a 'slice of life', realist writing depends as much as any other on a series of complex techniques, all of which have been borrowed by the avant-garde. Whatever kind of fiction you want to write – fantasy, metafiction, horror or science fiction – you will need to entice your readers with the strengths of good realist writing: immediacy, convincing characters and credible places and plots.

Here is an example from Pat Barker's *Union Street*, often seen as – and wrongly disparaged for – merely reflecting what its first blurb writer called 'the grit, the humour, the reality of working-class life'.

In the following lines 11-year-old Kelly looks at the man who has raped her. Note how Barker's language excludes rather than embraces the everyday detail of the chip shop in which this scene is set:

> Something was happening to his face. It was beginning to split, to crack, to disintegrate from within, like an egg when the time for hatching has come. She wanted to run. She didn't want to stay there and see what would hatch out of this egg. But horror kept her pinned to her chair. And the face went on cracking. And now moisture of some kind was oozing out of the corners of his eyes, running into cracks that had not been there a minute before, dripping, finally, into the open, the agonised mouth. (Barker, 1982, p. 33)

Barker's challenge is to convey distress and injustice from the viewpoint of a girl too young fully to comprehend or explain it. Unlike Thomas Hardy in his *Tess of the d'Urbervilles*, the narrator does not intervene to discuss the evils of rape. Yet her scrupulous adherence to Kelly's point of view (abandoned elsewhere) implicitly makes her allegiance known. Through her extended simile-cum-metaphor – the rapist's face as cracking egg – Barker disrupts or 'defamiliarizes' his tears of what we presume are guilt and self-disgust, thus recovering a horror which for the adult reader might otherwise have been blunted. The writing offers us a vision as stylized and grotesque as that of a scene from the stories of Angela Carter. *JN*

redrafting

What we do to turn what we first produce into what we can develop no further. Anne Lamott (1995) writes inspiringly about how 'really shitty first drafts' can be turned into something of which you can be proud. For anyone who calls him- or herself a writer, drafting and redrafting is what it is all about. Many writers regard redrafting as a pleasure – Raymond Carver, for instance: 'There's not much that I like better than to take a story that I've had around the house for a while and work it over again' (quoted in Charters, 1995). *RG*

reflective writing

Writing in which you articulate and record your thoughts about what you read and what you write, about the kind of writer you are and the kind of writer you would like to become. You may examine your own creative processes, as Iris Murdoch does here:

> I plan the whole thing in detail before I begin. I have a general scheme and lots of notes. Every chapter is planned. Every conversation is planned. (Plimpton, 1992, p. 120)

In reflecting about your work, you may make it more real to yourself as a writer; you will become more self-aware and self-critical and develop faster as a writer. Remember Socrates: the unexamined life is not worth living. Part of the rationale of reflective writing is that the artist who stops to consider what he or she is doing will probably end up doing it better.

Perhaps the most significant thing to remember about reflective writing is that it begins by you making the choice to think on the page. Bear in mind E. M. Forster's telling observation: 'How do I know what I think until I see what I say?' Start by asking yourself questions about your work. What were your intentions with this piece? Have you fulfilled them? Will the reader always be fully engaged? What obstacles faced you while you were writing the piece? What were your strategies for overcoming them? How successful were these strategies? How did your reading influence you?

To be self-critical, you will need to examine your work carefully and probably at some distance. If you look at your work fresh from writing it, you won't be able to see the wood for the trees. Besides, most of us at the moment of finishing something tend to think that it is good.

Reflective writing is more than just self-criticism, though. You will often use your writer's journal to record thoughts you have about work in progress. Just the other day a novel I was reading featured some racist abuse and it occurred to me that in the novel I am writing a particular dispute might be enhanced by giving it a racist inflection. So I wrote the idea down, a note to self. Another form of reflection is to keep a process log, in which you record the many changes a piece of work goes through. Here you will be thinking on paper or screen about what you are doing, which will help you come up with alterations you might like to make. Keeping a process log will encourage you to rationalize and theorize your strategies, in the manner of Vicki Feaver here:

> I wrote out draft after draft of the opening, the details building gradually. The adjective 'long' was added to the hair, not just adding a detail to the picture but the repeated 'l's and the three stressed single-syllable words ('long oiled hair') lengthening and slowing up the line. (Bell and Magrs, 2001, p. 285)

From this, you may end up articulating a philosophy of composition, a writer's manifesto, as Lorrie Moore has done:

> One must listen and proceed, sentence to sentence, hearing what comes next in one's story – which can be a little maddening. It can be like trying to understand a whisper in a foreign accent: did she say *Je t'adore* or *Shut the door*? (Boylan, 1993, p. 202)

In order to turn yourself into a reflective practitioner, it's a good idea to get into the habit of writing evaluatively about each piece of creative work you produce. If you need to justify this to yourself, remember that such self-evaluation is a terrific aid to redrafting. However, there can be a great deal more to this kind of discourse than looking for ways of improving the work. Here you may discuss any creative or theoretical work which informed the writing. You may consider your use of particular elements of craft: **flashback** or **dialogue**, for instance. You might discuss the literary context into which you think your work might fit. Writing about each piece of creative work you produce will contribute to making you more self-conscious, more self-critical, as well as giving you a better understanding of the kind of writer you are.

Let me finish by showering you with a list of some aspects of writing reflectively. You may consider inspiration or intention. You may write about the genesis of the work and any reading that informed it. You might write a process log or a self-evaluation of a piece of creative work. You could look at your working methods and any difficulties encountered along the way. You could reflect about your use of craft and about the redrafting. You could examine your own creative processes, or think about any literary context to which you might belong. Whatever you reflect about in writing, you should look at it the way you look at physical exercise. It won't always feel easy, but it will always be beneficial. *RG*

Writing ideas
1. *A reflection*
   Choose a short story you have written. Now see if you can produce 500 words of reflection about it. This reflection may consider: the original idea and how you developed it; your influences; the effects you hoped to have on the reader; problems encountered during the writing and your strategies for overcoming them; the drafting process; what you have learned in the production of this piece. A bibliography of any texts that informed the writing is always a good idea.
2. *A reading log*
   Reflecting about what you read is as beneficial as reflecting about your own writing, so you might like to keep a reading log. Begin by writing a 500-word piece of reflective writing about a book you are reading. Make notes on passages you admire, analysing the skills the author uses and the effects their use have on the reader. Break down the attributes of the author's style. Express in writing why this novel appealed to you. Finally, write about what can be learned from studying this passage.

Writing reflectively about your work and keeping a reading log should be a way of life for you.

Further reading

Bell, Julia and Paul Magrs (eds), *The Creative Writing Coursebook* (London: Macmillan, 2001).

Boylan, Clare (ed.), *The Agony and The Ego* (London: Penguin, 1993).

Plimpton, George (ed.), *The Writer's Chapbook* (New York, Penguin, 1992).

rejection

Like love, it hurts. There are many apocryphal stories of famous writers papering their walls with rejection slips, of great books being turned away by publisher after publisher until finally being recognized as a work of genius: Nobel prize-winner William Golding's *Lord of The Flies* is one of those often mentioned. These stories can give heart and hope to those who believe their work to be unjustly cast aside, but before you decide a publisher or agent is an idiot, and once you've got over the burning rage and shame that often accompanies rejection, it's worth considering why.

You may have sent it to the wrong person or publisher. Save time and trouble by reading their guidelines for submission, either on their website or in *The Writer's Handbook*. Never send unsolicited manuscripts if they ask you not to: it won't get looked at and you're wasting money on postage. Your work may not be ready, needing more revision, or it may not be considered marketable at this time by that particular agent or publisher. The most useful rejections are those that give reasons and make suggestions as to how the work might be improved.

Don't be too blasé about rejections, try to learn from them, but don't let yourself be put off, either. It is a hard world out there for writers, and although you may need to lick your wounds for a while, don't wait too long before you're sending work off again. To infinity and beyond!   *HL*

Further reading
Golding, William, *Lord of the Flies* (London: Faber, 1997).
Turner, Barry, *The Writer's Handbook* (London: Macmillan, produced annually, latest edition).

repetition

Repetition of sound, syllable, word and phrase has been a key characteristic of poetry for centuries. It is used in **fixed form** poetry involving repetition of lines and in poems with a chorus, such as ballads**.** Repetition contributes to the musicality of poetry, helping to create a **rhythm** through sonic or **phonemic patterns**. It also creates emphasis, drawing attention to key phrases or words. Look at Ted Hughes' use of repetition in 'Song of a Rat'. The opening line, 'The rat is in the trap, it is in the trap', immediately sets up a sense of urgency and pain through repetition of words and sounds. Some believe that intense repetition, in primitive chanting, as well as in modernist experimentation, may induce a mystical trance-like experience.   *HT*

Further reading
Hughes, Ted, *New Selected Poems 1957–1994* (London: Faber and Faber, 1995).

research

Finding out about things. The most fundamental form of research for writers is reading. If you are trying to write a novel, you should be fully conversant with contemporary practice. Related to this is the research you should do into the market for which you want to write. Which books are selling well? Which are winning prizes? Which publishers are putting out books like the one you are writing?

Finally, your writing will sometimes require you to cover subject matter about which you know little or nothing. Dickens would have had to have done some research on extended court cases to write *Bleak House*, and no doubt Sebastian Faulks knew more about the First World War after writing *Birdsong* than before. RG

(See also **data**)

revision

Looking at your work again and seeing how it may be developed and improved. It involves evaluating your work and is about bigger, broader, deeper things than editing. The roots of the word 'revise' suggest seeing again, and as you do so, your increased understanding of your work may prompt all sorts of alterations. In editing, you might take things out or correct, but in revision you might move words around, alter or expand them. Revision helps you not only to change existing writing but often to write new material.

Revision may mean altering the way characters have been rendered because now, further into the enterprise, you have come to understand them better than you did at first draft stage. Characters are created as you write, so when reading a first draft, you will notice things you hadn't before. In taking a step back, you will come to understand your characters better and, with this greater understanding, you will know what is and what it not characteristic of each one of them; you will know more precisely what they will and what they will not say and do. 'Characters', John Gardner advises, 'must stand before us with a wonderful clarity, such continuous clarity that nothing they do strikes us as improbable behaviour for just that character' (Gardner, 1991, p. 45). As you read and revise, you will take out details that do not belong, thus strengthening the characterization. Somebody once spoke of sculpture as a matter of removing all the pieces of the raw stone that don't belong. Because characters continue to evolve as you study each draft, as well as taking details out, you will also add some that reinforce or develop them. Your characters are not created in one draft, but in many. Oakley Hall mentions Richard Price taking two years to write his novels 'of which the first is spent living with his characters' (Hall, 1989, p. 42).

Another way to develop your characters is to look at the relationships between them. It can be very helpful to think of one character as a foil for another. If one sister is soft-hearted and gentle, and the other harsh and critical, it will enhance the characterization of both to make each a little more emphatically delineated. In this way, you differentiate between them more and the resulting stark contrast will enhance the characterization of both. You can also look for ways to turn the difference between the two into a source of conflict. A liberal man may be married to a puritanical woman and the resulting friction ought to be a source of useful tension.

As you read and revise, read and revise, you will come to understand your characters, the differences between them and the resulting tensions better. As a result, you will be able to revise your plot. 'If you aspire to a book that will last,' says Hilary Mantel, 'don't think about plot at all, think about your characters' (in Boylan (ed.), 1993, p. 38). Once you know your protagonist inside out, you will be able to see what she would do in any given situation. This will mean that parts of the first draft plot will have to go, but in the main it ought to suggest the almost inevitable direction of the plot – because characters can't help being characteristic.   *RG*

Writing idea
Find a first draft you have written and

1. carefully prune all clutter and then
2. remove everything superfluous from it.

Feels good, doesn't it?

Further reading
Boylan, Clare (ed.), *The Agony and The Ego: The Art and Strategy of Fiction Writing Explored* (London: Penguin, 1993).
Gardner, John, *The Art of Fiction: Notes on Craft for Young Writers* (New York: Vintage Books, 1991).
Hall, Oakley, *The Art & Craft of Novel Writing* (Cincinnati: Story Press, 1989).

rhyme

The most famous (some would say infamous) **phonemic pattern** in Western poetry is rhyme, seen by many as a defining characteristic of the genre, although it is a much later development in English verse than **metre**, **alliteration** and **repetition**. Rhyming words begin with differing consonants, but have similar sounding medial vowels and final consonants. It is the sound (the phonemes) not the spelling that matters: 'lawn' can happily rhyme with 'porn', for example. Rhyming words are usually found at the ends of lines.

One of the oldest forms of rhyme is the couplet, in which two adjacent lines rhyme, but there are infinite rhyming possibilities. The conventional system for referring to these is an alphabetical one, the first rhyming pair deemed to be 'a' and the second 'b' and so on. A four-line stanza with interlacing rhymes (subsequent lines ending in 'lawn', 'spring', 'porn' and 'fling') would be described as 'abab'.

Rhyme is much used in popular poetry, from greetings cards to humorous verse to children's poetry, but although some 'serious' poets employ set rhyme schemes, many regard them as over-restrictive and forced. There is the danger that your reader will overemphasize your rhyming at the expense of the overall sound and meaning. Clichéd rhyme, or the pairing of two ill-fitting words in order to achieve a rhyme, can be distressing, but an original rhyme can be impressive, especially if it challenges expectations. See Norman MacCaig's poem 'Summer Farm' for a striking example of a structured poem, written in rhyming couplets using simple rhymes such as 'grass/glass' and 'see/me' to powerful effect.

The key for a new writer is to develop subtlety and courage: break the rules; miss out a rhyme; substitute a half-rhyme (such as 'laugh' and 'life') or an internal rhyme (rhyming words in the middle and at the end of a line). For ideas and inspiration, read and listen to 'Talking Turkeys' by the reggae poet, Benjamin Zephaniah, whose use of rhyme such as: 'hip hop' with 'de chop'; 'mass' with 'cash'; and 'Humans get greedy and waste more dan need be' demonstrate flamboyance and wit.   *HT*

Further reading

MacCaig, Norman, *Collected Poems* (London: Chatto and Windus, 1990).

Zephaniah, Benjamin, 'Talking Turkeys' read out loud by him at www.bbc.co.uk/arts/poetry/outloud (accessed 14 December 2006).

rhythm

The beat of your words. May be created through the way hard and soft sounds are knitted together in a sentence. Sibilance, **assonance** and **alliteration**, too, will affect the rhythm. Longer sentences offer more opportunities to vary the rhythm and to build musicality. In poetry, rhythm and metre may be one and the same. In fiction and scriptwriting, dialogue depends to some extent on rhythm. Pound advised Hemingway to be faithful to the rhythms of natural speech, which is not as straightforward as merely recording what people say. A good way to check the rhythm of your writing is to read it aloud.   *RG*

(See also **metre and rhythm**)

romance plot

As far back as the twelfth century, Marie de France was turning out courtly soap operas about the glamorous affairs of knights and damsels. There has always been a huge appetite for romance literature, whether it's Mills and Boon or Jane Austen. And therefore it's worth considering what a romance plot can add to your work, even if you weren't aspiring to be the next Barbara Cartland. There are lots of resources to help the budding romance writer. Mills and Boon have an extensive website, which contains a useful advice section for would-be authors (an indication of the volume of submissions they receive). Sheri McGregor, romantic novelist, also provides some helpful 'how to' advice, which can be found on ehow.com.

A suitable hero and heroine are especially important in the romance plot. The whole point of the book is that they are meant to be together, and the reader follows them through obstacles and complications until the happy ending where all is resolved. Jane Austen is the oft-cited example of this sort of story. The hero and heroine need to be worthy of the reader's interest, the kind of people who deserve happiness. But they can't be too perfect or too good-looking: the reader needs to relate to them, not envy them. So a judicious sprinkling of misfortune never goes amiss. And minor flaws, such as being too proud, too feisty or too guarded, help the plot along as our hero and heroine learn things about themselves and change their attitudes accordingly before they can reap their reward at the end.   *UH*

Further reading

Austen, Jane, *The Complete Novels of Jane Austen* (Ware: Wordsworth Editions Ltd, 2005).

De France, Marie, *French Mediaeval Romances From The Lays Of Marie De France* (London: Kessinger Publishing Co., 2004).

McGregor, Sheri, 'How to Plot a Romance Novel', www.ehow.com/how_16764_plot-romance-novel.html (accessed 14 December 2006).

Mills and Boon: www.millsandboon.co.uk.

Romanticism

The name given to a creative revolution that transformed Western art and literature in the late eighteenth and early nineteenth centuries and which is still influential today. The Romantic movement, in reaction to a more restrictive and hierarchical period, emphasized individual expression, originality and spontaneity, which are all self-evidently good things, but which have their

downsides for the contemporary writer. Three self-defeating Romantic ideas are that you need to live somewhere rural and dramatic like the Villa Diodati on Lake Geneva rather than Crewe; that to be a true genius you need to die tragically young like Percy Shelley; and that you have to be 'inspired' to write. It's useful to remember that J. R. R. Tolkien was brought up in Birmingham; that Shakespeare died in his bed; and that Jack London said writers shouldn't wait for inspiration, but 'go after it with a club'.   *HL*
(See also **block** and **imagination**)

room

Virginia Woolf famously said that 'a woman must have money and a room of her own if she is to write fiction', both of which may be hard to come by for a writer of either sex who lives in the average shoebox-sized dwelling with a mortgage or rent to pay. Quiet and privacy are important in order to develop the creative state of mind that comes when you get deeply into your writing. It's also helpful to read your work aloud sometimes so that you can hear how it sounds, and this feels silly if you're in earshot of other people. Anne Dillard worked for a time in an eight- by ten-foot tool shed with a desk, shelf, chair and bed and not much of a view. As she says,

> Appealing workplaces are to be avoided. Once I wrote in a cinder-block cell over a parking lot. One wants a room with no view, so imagination can meet memory in the dark. (Dillard, 1989, p. 26)

HL

Further reading

Dillard, Anne, *The Writing Life* (New York: Harper Perennial, 1990).
Woolf, Virginia, *A Room of One's Own* (London: Penguin, 2004).

scenes

Something happening, live. A script is built on scenes, as is a novel. Scenes in fiction depend on **immediacy** and are thus always shown, not told. Scenes move forward through **action** and **dialogue** and make clear what the setting is. The screenwriter William Goldman advises that 'We must enter all scenes as late as possible. We must enter our story as late as possible' (Goldman, 2000, p. 198). Whatever the situation at the start of a scene, it ought to have noticeably changed by the end. Scenes may end with a reversal. In the book of Esther in the Bible, one of the scenes ends with Haman being hung on the gallows he had had built for his adversary Mordecai. *RG*

Further reading

Goldman, William, *Which Lie Did I Tell?* (London: Bloomsbury, 2000), p. 198.

scriptwriting

Writing, usually narrative in type, for live performance on stage, or recorded performance on screen, TV or radio. Each medium is distinct in its requirements and forms, and whether it be television, film, radio or live theatre performance, each generates another long list of genres particular to it: there are television dramas, soap operas, series, serials, sitcoms . . . and the same goes for film and radio and theatre. It surely goes without saying, then, that the writer must be more than familiar with the medium and the genres therein. However, if you want to write, for example, a screenplay, it is not enough to watch a lot of films: you must explore them with a screenwriter's eye, analysing the writer's techniques in terms of genre-specific narrative structure and character development in both visual and aural terms. You must also *read* a lot of screenplays (or stage plays, or radio scripts). Merely watching, however detailed your analysis, is like learning how to draw up architectural blueprints by examining finished buildings, when, in fact, the best thing you can do is to look at a lot of other people's blueprints. In this way you build up a strong working vocabulary of the conventions that adhere to each genre.

And as for conventions or 'rules': if you're going to change the face of, say, film-making by doing it completely differently, and for that matter bigger and better (and I've heard it said), it's best to understand the conventions of a medium and its genres before you set foot in it and smash up its crockery and its rules. But by all means push the boundaries: this is how writers and forms develop. The rules are, after all, only guidelines, and slavish devotion to unbreakable regulations is as treacherous a course of action as arrogantly ignoring every single principle. If you passionately believe you can make something work, then go for it.

Scriptwriters, like other writers, keep notebooks and use them to record ideas, but also the fragments of heard dialogue too precious to lose: people say the funniest, strangest, most gorgeous things; catch them if you can. In capturing these fragments you'll immerse yourself in the idiosyncratic speech idioms which it can be all too easy to miss when you're writing characters. Try visiting places to watch and listen to people (without getting arrested): railway stations, cafés and art galleries are good communal spaces. You don't need to hear everything to get hooked into miniature situations; middles are enough. Let your imagination take over to give you beginnings and ends.

Lots of scriptwriters read their work aloud. It's written to be spoken, so speak it to help you make it speakable. As with fiction, the best plots come from character, and planning is part of the process, and remember that script work is about action and conflict in terms of time and space. So spend time building characters and getting to know how they behave before they open their mouths.

A script that works in one medium does not necessarily work in another: some stories are born to be film narratives; others are theatre narratives. The rhythms of each medium are different. There is crossover, but if you analyse closely films such as *Closer* and *Twelve Angry Men* you'll note that they feature long, complex exchanges of dialogue between small numbers of characters in the same location. It should therefore come as no big surprise to learn that they began their lives as stage plays. If you do your script analysis work often enough, you'll begin to get a feel for which narrative is best told in which medium. And learn how to format correctly: nothing screams 'amateur!' as loudly as a badly laid-out script. Don't forget that the first contact your script has is with a reader; so help them read it.

scriptwriting

Theatre is a symbolic medium in that it often visually suggests rather than represents. The physical realities of shifting vast amounts of furniture in between scenes, and the financial constraints of affording lots of actors can be seen as a limitation or a liberation depending on the way your dramatic imagination works, but multiple realistic locations and casts of thousands tend not to be the lingua franca of contemporary theatre. Modern stage design often offers symbolic visual representations of internal emotions and notions so that characters walk through abstract constructions that enhance the themes and/or emotional journeys of the play. For examples, click on the gallery pages of the website of The Society of British Theatre Designers at www.theatredesign.org.uk. You'll see what a visually exciting and beautiful medium theatre is.

It almost goes without saying that film is also a highly visual medium, but it can be a neglected aspect of novice screenwriting. But think of the sumptuous visual spectacle of *The Last Emperor*, or the vast landscapes of *The Motorcycle Diaries*. Here, the landscapes and the *mise en scène* are an integral part of the stories. Film is a medium operating verisimilitudinally: that is to say that what we're shown is designed to look like reality, and great effort is made to replicate and/or fake it. Great effort is also made to design what we see: cinematography is a fundamental part of film-making: screen narratives that offer imaginative opportunities for this are highly valued. Look for stories set in visually interesting places. Let your story tell itself in visual terms. Not everything needs to be spoken to be conveyed to an audience.

Advice, blogs and more are to be found on several websites. Try Channel 4's website for *The Play's The Thing* at www.channel4.com/culture/microsites/T/the_play.

The BBC has an excellent website, The Writers' Room, offering free downloads of scriptwriting software, a script archive and news and advice. Find it at www.bbc.co.uk/writersroom.

There isn't space here to elucidate in the fine detail needed the specific features of writing for each medium, nor to mention the genres within that medium, so would-be scriptwriters must now read more widely: the books listed below are excellent starting points.   *HN*

Writing ideas

1. *Fragments*

   Listen to people talking. Discreetly take notes of what you overhear. (Be ethical. Don't draw attention to yourself, and don't do this if you have any doubts about your own safety!) You'll hear snippets of interesting/ banal/bizarre conversation on buses, in cafés, theatre foyers, dog tracks and/or chip shops. Analyse your results and compare them with the well-crafted conversations you hear in theatre plays, television soap operas and films. The conversations you collect might be full of non sequiturs or they might drift purposelessly; or they might drive into cul-de-sacs . . . I don't know what you'll find, but use what you find: craft the snippets into miniature scenes. Less is more here: no need to explain too much. Enjoy playing with intriguing your audience/reader.

2. *Monologues*

Talk into a Dictaphone. Try to keep talking for at least ten minutes, even longer if you can manage. Tell a joke. Tell a tale. Talk about the day you got fired. Talk about your first day at school. Just keep talking. Transcribe the results and compare the written monologue with how you would have crafted it in a script. No doubt the sentences would have been longer and more formal, and the clauses more complex in their links to one another. There's a lot more to writing a script than capturing the way people talk as opposed to write, but it's a damn fine place to start.

Further reading

Goldman, William, *Adventures in the Screen Trade* (London: Abacus, 1996).

Hatcher, Jeffrey, *The Art and Craft of Playwriting* (Cincinnati: Writers' Digest Books, 2000).

McGrath, Declan, *Screenwriting* (Hove: RotoVision, 2003).

McKee, Robert, *Story: Substance, Structure and Style and the Principles of Screen-writing* (London: Methuen, 1999).

Mamet, David, *Three Uses of the Knife: On the Nature and Purpose of Drama* (London: Vintage, 2000).

Taylor, Val, *Stage Writing: A Practical Guide* (Ramsbury: Crowood Press, 2002).

section-breaks

Spaces between scenes or sections. The simplest way to understand a section-break is to see it as a slighter version of the break between chapters. It is indicated on the page by leaving an extra line at the end of a particular section and by not indenting the first line of the following section. Often these sections are scenes, but they may sometimes consist of several scenes. The use of section-breaks divides book-length prose into units smaller than chapters. In short stories, section-breaks perhaps take the place of chapter divisions. As with chapters, the section-break acknowledges both that narratives have particular movements and that readers welcome breaks to give their minds a rest.   *RG*

self-publishing

Otherwise known as vanity publishing, which is an indication of the esteem in which it is held in some, or many, quarters. You will see plenty of organizations advertising in the classified sections of Sunday broadsheets and in the writing magazines, offering to help you get published. You can assume they are in it for the money, and in the first instance the money is yours. Mainstream publishers are also in it for the money but the money is the reader's. As a result, most self-publishing firms will offer you little support in getting the boxfuls of books from your garage and onto the shelves of your readers.

An exception might be if you have written a book which has only a very limited market, such as a family history which you simply long to see bound in print. In this case, it will be far cheaper to send your script to a printer (far easier in the word-processed age) and pay them directly. Unlike a vanity publisher, they won't charge you a fee for false promises and hollow praise.

By and large, don't do it. If we can assume that writers write because they have something to say to the rest of the world – a story that someone else thinks is worth listening to – why publish yourself? The likelihood is that you are writing for yourself and only being enjoyed by yourself. There's a word for that.*

There are notable exceptions but these can probably be taken to prove the rule and you should only resort to self-publishing if you are prepared to pound the streets trying to get booksellers to put your books on their shelves, then call on every literary editor in the country and pester them into reviewing your book. In all likelihood, these will result in rejections equally as dispiriting as those from agents and publishers which have driven you to self-publishing in the first place.   *GC*
(*Diarist)

sentence

A unit of language, often containing a subject, a verb and an object: *Suzanne* (subject) *drank* (verb) *her coffee* (object). The first thing to say about sentences is that, most of the time, they should *be* sentences. Here are two sentences: *This is a sentence. A short sentence.* The first is a grammatically correct sentence; the second is not, mainly because it lacks a verb. Both, however, are acceptable because a technically ungrammatical sentence has been used for reasons of style. The following is not a sentence and is unacceptable. *Many people head off to the sun at this time of year, I've been known to take a holiday in June myself.* Really, that should have been two sentences, although inserting a semicolon after 'year' would have made it work. Why is one non-sentence permissible and the other not? Perhaps because the author in the former seemed to know what he was doing, but in the latter that was clearly not the case.

Except perhaps for emphases and rhythm, sentences ought to be devoid of the superfluous. In the following sentence, the final three words are not only repetitive, they're superfluous. *The hall was already full by the time they got there and Terry cursed herself for taking so long to get there.*

In your use of language, the selection of vocabulary and the way you construct sentences are the two broad strategies available to you. One school of thought prefers sentences that are concise and economical.

In the twentieth century, the great proponent of this approach to sentence construction was Hemingway: 'The sun was coming up over the hills. A bass jumped, making a circle in the water. Nick trailed his hand in the water.' (From the story 'Indian Camp'.) All the evidence is that Hemingway took to heart Ezra Pound's advice to use absolutely no word that does not contribute to the general design.

Taut and tight is not the only option, though. Longer sentences offer more opportunities to vary the rhythm and to build musicality. A sentence that extends for line after line without losing your attention can be enthralling. Many contemporary writers, such as Margaret Atwood or Richard Ford, favour sentences that are not only longer but also more lavish and lush, like Salman Rushdie's here:

> While I sit like an empty pickle jar in a pool of Anglepoised light, visited by this vision of my grandfather sixty-three years ago, which demands to be recorded, filling my nostrils with the acrid stench of his mother's embarrassment which has brought her out in boils, with the vinegary force of Aadam Aziz's determination to establish a practice so successful that she'll never have to return to the gemstone-shop, with the blind mustiness of a big shadowy house in which the young Doctor stands, ill-at-ease, before a painting of a plain girl with lively eyes and a stag

transfixed behind her on the horizon, speared by a dart from her bow. (Rushdie, 1995, p. 19)

There's a place for both approaches – even within the work of one writer.

RG

Writing idea

Write a page about the last new place you visited. In it, vary the length of your sentences as much as you can. Here's a suggested approach: first paragraph, short sentences; second paragraph, medium length sentences; third paragraph, a mixture of short, medium length and long sentences. Once you've completed the page, read it aloud and assess the effect of the different kinds of sentence length.

Further reading

Hemingway, Ernest, *The Short Stories: The First Forty-Nine Stories* (New York: Simon & Schuster, 1995).

Rushdie, Salman, *Midnight's Children* (London: Vintage, 1995).

setting

The place or the era where fiction happens. Your writing may not make setting as prominent a feature as Dickens' London or Hardy's Wessex, but setting is important in all writing. If it is to have any solidity, much creative writing – fiction and memoir, certainly, and scriptwriting probably – needs to happen somewhere. Fiction that has no sense of place has a thin, empty feel to it and, to put it more positively, sometimes the sense of place in a book can be as significant as the characters. I've mentioned Dickens' London and Hardy's Wessex, but what about the Fens in Graham Swift's *Waterland* or the sea in Patrick O'Brian's novels? In all these examples, the setting has been foregrounded and plays an important part in the effect of the work on the reader.

Setting should complement character and plot to make the world of your story more vivid for the reader. It can illuminate character, as Philip Marlowe's office does in Raymond Chandler's detective fiction. Protagonists in fiction usually have a relationship with the setting in which they are found. Sometimes – in Cormac McCarthy's *All the Pretty Horses*, for instance – this will be a congenial relationship, but often protagonists are at odds with their setting, as Holden Caulfield is with New York in *The Catcher in the Rye*. Such tension between character and setting helps to reveal the character but may also advance the plot, as the asylum where Sue Trinder is incarcerated in Sarah Waters' *Fingersmith* does.

The following extract from *Birdsong* by Sebastian Faulks gives an indication of the part that setting can play in fiction.

> Each sandbag was three feet long and two feet across. They had been packed densely with what Jack called spoil, the debris of digging, in order to maximise their ability to contain the blast. With only one good hand to pull them, Stephen worked very slowly, each drag of about six inches followed by a rest.
>
> He talked to Jack as he worked, hoping that his voice would stop him from slipping way. There was no response from the figure slumped on the ground. Although progress was measured in inches, he worked with a fury given him by hope. He had a picture in his mind of a great crater being blown into the field above them, and of him and Jack emerging from behind their shelter of sandbags to walk into the bottom of it, which, though thirty feet below ground level, would be open to the rain and the wind.
>
> He was able to stand up in the enlarged area of tunnel and stretch his back from time to time. Each time he rested he bent over Jack and tried to rouse him with a mixture of force and cajoling. There was usually some response, though it was grudging and incoherent; he seemed to be delirious again.
>
> Stephen went back to his work. He switched off the torch and laboured in the darkness. When he had cleared a dozen bags and stacked them in the main tunnel, it became easier to work because there was more space around him. He wanted to stop and make sure Jack was still all right, but feared that the more time he wasted by not clearing the bags, the closer they would come to the end of Jack's life.
>
> He pressed on. (Faulks, 1994, pp. 471–2)

Here the protagonist is clearly at odds with his setting. The struggle he has in fighting his way, inch by inch, out of this place comes across repeatedly. The oppressiveness of the setting – a tunnel at the front in the First World War – is as important to this passage as the character. It's hard to be there, and escaping is a painful activity – the difficulty of moving comes across clearly, as does the claustrophobic situation Stephen is in. The setting resists Stephen's efforts to advance, which creates much of the narrative tension. (The rest arises from the race against time to break through before Jack dies.) Remove the setting and you are left with two characters, one of whom is dying. The setting adds greatly to our sense of Stephen's perilous condition and the opposition it presents to his will. It reveals Stephen's character; the immovability of the earth that traps him gives us the chance to see how determined and strong he is.

Sometimes setting may be used to dramatize, to make an already tense situation much more dramatic. In Rose Tremain's novel *The Way I Found Her*, we see her protagonist Lewis on rooftops several times during the course of the narrative. The climax of the novel comes when he and Valentina, the woman he loves, have to escape the men who have kidnapped them. It's already a dramatic situation that Lewis has to save himself and Valentina; making the escape include a climb over rooftops and a leap from one roof to another raises the ante, however, making the situation even more fraught. (And this peak is enhanced by the author's having shown us throughout the novel that Lewis is good on a rooftop.) More than anything, it is the setting that makes this a climactic moment:

> So all I did was smile and stroke Valentina's arm, and then I gathered all my strength and all my courage and I turned away from her and round towards the sunrise and leapt outwards and felt the air underneath me buoy me up away from the pull of gravity and land me, still upright, on the corrugated iron roof of the barn.
>
> I let myself topple forwards. The iron was rusty and harsh on my bare feet, but it didn't buckle or split. A feeling of elation began stabbing at me, stronger than anything I seemed to have known. I wanted to yell, 'I did it! I did it!' I wanted to dance about on the iron like a voodoo spirit. (Tremain, 1998, p. 346)

Your setting is not fixed and unchangeable, of course, and if it's outside, the weather can change. This is **pathetic fallacy**. Rain at a funeral will add to the sorrow of the occasion, while sunshine will contrast with it. Using pathetic fallacy to add to the emotional tone of a scene is probably more normal, though – you will often find a storm used to exaggerate an emotional storm going on between two characters, although this may come across as a **cliché**.

A quick final word: setting more often than not is another word for place, but do remember that the setting of a piece of fiction may be the *time* that it is set in. So, to go with someone just mentioned, Sarah Waters' first three novels are set in Victorian England and her most recent during the Second World War. Much of what I've said above will also apply to the era in which a novel is set.   *RG*

Writing ideas

1. *Seaside town*

    Most of us have had a holiday in a seaside town. Take a piece of paper and brainstorm on just such a seaside town. List all the attributes of the place you can think of (seaweed, smell of salt water, ice cream cones, buckets and spades, luminous plastic necklaces, windbreak, paddling, the promenade, kiss-me-quick hats). Now think of someone you know reasonably well – it might be you – who would really hate having to spend any time in such a place. Write a story in which he or she takes an aged relative there for a weekend.

2. *Restaurant reunion*

    Two couples, A & B and C & D, are eating together in a restaurant. A and D used to be lovers and tonight, as the wine flows, the spark between them is rekindled. Write about how this develops as the evening progresses. A public setting such as a restaurant can be used to notch up the drama here.

Further reading

Faulks, Sebastian, *Birdsong* (London: Vintage, 1994).
Tremain, Rose, *The Way I Found Her* (London: Vintage, 1998).
Waters, Sarah, *The Night Watch* (London: Virago, 2006).

sex

Writing a sex scene can be scary. Is it too much? Is it enough? Will it be ridiculed? Will your mother read it? There is huge pressure on a writer to include sex in their work. And sex does sell. There's money to be made in pornographic and erotic writing. Writers like Anne Rice earned a living doing this before hitting the big time with more mainstream work. Of course, different genres require different approaches, but there are some basic principles that apply across the board. First of these, according to Steve Almond, is to stop having sex. 'Remember that the sexiest thing about sex is really desire, which is just a fancy word for not getting laid' (Almond, 2003).

The best sex scenes rely on the most erotic organ of them all: the brain.

Hint and innuendo, intrigue and suggestion create space for the reader's imagination to quite literally do the dirty work for you. It's the dance of the seven veils versus a Page 3 lovely. The safest ploy is to 'do a Jane Austen' and discreetly close the bedroom door. Other writers give us a bare statement of fact, and leave our imaginations to do the rest. Here's an example from Chinua Achebe's *Things Fall Apart*:

> It had been early in the morning. The moon was shining. She was going to the stream to fetch water. Okonkwo's house was on the way to the stream. She went in and knocked at his door and he came out. Even in those days he was not a man of many words. He just carried her into his bed and in the darkness began to feel around her waist for the loose end of her cloth. (Achebe, 2001, p. 80)

This description is coolly detached, dignified. We know what is going to happen; Achebe need do no more.

On other occasions, it is necessary to go into more detail – not for gratuitous titillation, but because it is clearly required for the development of character and plot. Here's an example from Marek Halter's *Sarah*:

> Abram took the hem of the shawl and lifted it. She did not move. They looked at each other while his hand rose to Sarai's temple and his fingers slid down her cheek to the nape of her neck. She stopped trembling.
> He smiled.
> He slid her dress off her, and she was naked. He moved back as though he were afraid to touch her. A moan came from his mouth. His tunic fell at once, and he, too, was naked.
> Sarai laid her fingers on the smooth skin at the base of his neck. The pulse was throbbing so rapidly that her fingers trembled. Abram shivered under her caress. Sarai's knees gave way, and Abram lay down with her on the rugs, his lips on hers. (Halter, 2004, pp. 138–9)

This writing sizzles with sexual tension, and yet there is no mention of X-rated body parts or biological processes. Halter gives us intimacy and sympathy with the characters' emotions (crucial in a romance plot), but most importantly knows when to stop. If in doubt, leave it out! *UH*

Writing ideas

From stark to soft focus

Sketch out a sex scene between two (or more) people. Think about character and motivation. Are they furtive, guilty, triumphant, ecstatic? What's going on here? Use the scene to communicate as much information about your characters as possible. Now rewrite the scene in different styles: understated; statement of fact; romantically embellished. Remember, you are not writing a biology text book.

Further reading

Achebe, Chinua, *Things Fall Apart* (London: Penguin Classics, 2001).
Almond, Steve, 'Writing Sex', *Boston Phoenix*, 25 April 2003.
Halter, Marek, *Sarah* (London: Bantam, 2004).

sexuality

A key component of our emotional and psychological make-up, and therefore a crucial aspect of character and motivation. Trying to conjure a convincing sexuality for a character is challenging. With whom do they choose/choose not to have sex? Why? What are the consequences of this? You've only got to look at the popular press to see that people are fascinated by the sexuality of others, especially the rich and famous. If you can get people equally fascinated by the sexuality of your imaginary characters, then you're well on your way to a successful piece of work.

Does it matter whether Henry James was gay? Virginia Woolf a lesbian? You bet! People have made careers out of trying to prove whether writers were homosexual. In fact these days the sexuality of the author can be a big selling point. Sarah Waters has done very well with her heady mixture of Victorian crime and girl-on-girl action. Alan Hollinghurst won the 2004 Booker Prize with *The Line of Beauty*, a tale of gay lust in Thatcher's 80s. Victorian crime and Thatcherite Britain have both been done before. It's the sexuality of the characters involved that makes them intriguing and therefore widely read. And no entry on sexuality would be complete without mentioning Annie Proulx's gay cowboy love story *Brokeback Mountain*. Make sexuality a major aspect of your characterization, and you could give your work the edge it needs.   *UH*

Further reading

Hollinghurst, Alan, *The Line of Beauty* (Basingstoke: Picador, 2005).
Proulx, Annie, *Close Range: Wyoming Stories* (London: Fourth Estate, 1999).
Waters, Sarah, *Fingersmith* (London: Virago, 2005).

short story

The short story often suffers in comparison with the novel: being seen by some writers and critics as a practice run, the first course before the superior main meal. Jonathan Franzen disagrees:

> A high percentage of the most exciting fiction written in the last 25 years . . . has been short fiction . . . I like stories because they leave the writer no place to hide. There's no yakking your way out of trouble. (Franzen, Introduction to Munrow, 2006).

A story doesn't have to have a conventional shape or form: it can be a list, a mosaic, a spiral. However, each word must count and there is no time for decorative description, for dialogue that doesn't go anywhere, for the kind of philosophical discursiveness that novelists sometimes get away with.

How short is short? There is no specific designated length for a short story, except that it is shorter than a novella (under 20,000 words), and is therefore normally too short to be published in a book of its own. A fairly recent phenomenon has been an upsurge in the popularity of very short fiction, perhaps as a consequence of our time-starved culture, and a number of publishers have recognized the value of marketing fiction in an easily digestible form. In 2006, for example, Picador launched a series of pocket-sized books called shots, priced at only one pound and described in their blurb as 'ultimately disposable, the literary alternative to a magazine'.

Short doesn't have to mean very short: there are plenty of much longer examples of the form: Alice Munro, the Canadian writer, described as one of the best contemporary short-story writers in English, regularly produces work of between 30 and 60 pages long. And, whatever the length, concision and economy does not necessarily mean that a short story lacks complexity or depth: one small event can contain a world of significance.

It isn't easy to write a good short story but once you've written one it is easier to get it published. There are an increasing number of story-writing competitions and many magazines, mainstream and small circulation, provide a good opportunity for new and established writers.   *HL*

Writing ideas

Dave Eggers' identification of material which suits the very short story – *some small event* – is a useful hint towards developing ideas for stories of any length: a few words overheard on a bus; the man begging in a doorway who unexpectedly blows you a kiss as you toss him a coin; the UFO you spotted as a child that no one else saw. Use the suggestions above or find a small event of your own. Try writing a couple of 50-word stories to begin with; then have a go at the 500-word limit.

Further reading

Eggers, Dave, *How We Are Hungry* (London: Penguin, 2006).

Also see the very short stories online and Dave Eggers' article (2004) about them at books.guardian.co.uk/shortshortstories.

Franzen, Jonathan, 'Introduction', in Alice Munro, *Runaway* (London: Penguin, 2006).

showing/telling

(See **dramatization** and **immediacy**)

simile

An **image** which is a kind of **metaphor**. The only difference is that a simile states that a thing is *like* something else: *you are like a rock to me*; whereas a metaphor simply states that something *is* something else: *you are my rock*.

HL

simple linear plot

The world's most common plot structure, which Michael Baldwin, in *The Way To Write Short Stories* (London: Elm Tree, 1986), outlines roughly as follows. A person has a wish, desire or goal, the fulfilment of which meets a series of impediments. The impediments are overcome and the goal is achieved. Variations: the pursued aim is either unattainable or once attained not worthwhile; the protagonist fails to overcome the impediments – to comic effect, or to tragic effect; an impediment is established and nothing progresses until the very end of the story (the plot put off). Note that the simple linear only works if you can interest readers in the central character.

RG

single viewpoint

Story told from the vantage point of one character. There are clear advantages to writing single viewpoint fiction. It offers one central authority, which is perhaps less confusing than having more than one. Oakley Hall argues that 'A single point of view can be a powerful unifying factor in a piece of fiction' (Hall, 1989, p. 36). When the whole story is told from one person's perspective, it's possible to convey in some depth what your narrator's thoughts and feelings are about everything they go through in the course of the narrative. Single viewpoint arguably offers the reader a more cohesive experience and certainly absolves them from the need to prefer one narrator to another. It is consistent and there is no danger of the reader being confused about whose viewpoint they are in. Henry James believed that restricting a narrative to one viewpoint enhanced its intensity and immediacy.

RG

(See also **multiple viewpoint**)

Further reading

Hall, Oakley, *The Art and Craft of Novel Writing* (Cincinnati: Story Press, 1989).

skills

The writing techniques you have learned to use – or need to. In studying writing, it may be helpful to think of what you're doing as learning a portfolio of skills. For one thing, this breaks down the task of learning to be, for example, a novelist into a number of smaller tasks: learning to characterize, to write dialogue, to construct a plot. One of my students, writing about her development, said she felt she had slowly acquired a writer's toolbox, which she could dip into and select what she needed. Portfolio of skills, writer's toolbox – whatever you call it and whatever kind of writer you want to be – it's safe to assume that it will involve you in learning a number of skills. *RG*

software

There are now many software programs for writers, some of which may help some people. You are justified in thinking that the repetition of 'some' in the last sentence implies scepticism about their value, particularly for fiction writers and poets. They may help a little with organization and structure but writing has to happen at the interface between mind and culture, rather than through a formulaic process. However, the use of dedicated software for script layout is well established, and you can download a free version of *Script Smart* from the BBC Writers' Room website (www.bbc.co.uk/writersroom/scriptsmart) and use it to submit scripts to the BBC. The industry-standard script software is *Final Draft*, available for both Macs and PCs, which is widely used and recommended, although you have to pay for this one (available from www.finaldraft.com or Amazon). *HL*

sonnet

The sonnet, made famous by Shakespeare, is the most popular and enduring of all **fixed forms**, consisting of 14 lines composed in iambic pentameter, with a set rhyme scheme. The form enables the exploration of emotion and ideas with a three-part structure which includes an introductory section, a group of lines in which the idea or feeling is developed, and a turn or twist in the final couplet or tercet. Read Edna St Vincent Millay's 'Sonnets from an Ungrafted Tree' for some fine examples then try one for yourself. It's a good exercise in concise exploration of ideas and form, and your lover will be thrilled to receive one. *HT*

Further reading

St Vincent Millay, Edna, *Collected Poems* (New York/London: Harper and Row, 1956).

Shakespeare, William, *The Complete Sonnets and Poems* (Oxford: Oxford University Press, 2002).

spellcheck

Word-processing tools which point out textual errors and suggest corrections. Microsoft Word also checks your grammar if you wish. Spellchecks have become a necessity for most of us but you need to watch out for their blind spots, glitches and blips. The spellcheck won't help you with words that are correctly spelled but wrongly used, as in '*their* going out', or '*there* going out', which should, of course, be written, '*they're* going out'. Sorting your *theres*, *theirs* and *they'res* is your job, not the machine's. Another area of confusion is between different kinds of English (UK, US and Zimbabwean versions in my spellchecker), easily dealt with by switching to the appropriate one. Spellchecks also struggle with experimental language use and 'incorrect English' (e.g. dialect; slang; colloquialisms, etc.). Think of a spellcheck as servant, not master. It does a very good job and it saves you a lot of time but you have to treat it with respect. After you've run the spellcheck, proofread again. If you're not sure, use the good old-fashioned dictionary. *HL*

stereotype

Pathetic old men staring wistfully out of their lonely windows. Young women with nothing in their heads but sex and shopping. Black people who have music in their souls. Asian women forced into marriage. French people who drink wine and are better at sex than the English. American warmongers. Muslim terrorists. No. No. No. Stereotypes are *clichéd* characters. They are

temptingly easy to write because of their very familiarity. This is not to say that the above people and situations *can't* exist, only that interesting writing works both *with* and *across* the grain of stereotype. A good exercise is to make your own list then subvert it. A Frenchman living in England and looking for love but who is very bad at sex, for example.   *HL*
(See **caricature**)

story

Imagine, once upon a far-off time, a small group of barely human people huddled in a cave with only a small fire between them and the huge black darkness outside. Someone, perhaps a mother trying to distract her children from their fear of wolves and lions, began to tell a tale made up of actual remembered events mixed with pieces of dreams. As Richard Kearney says in *On Stories*,

> Once the listeners heard the beginning they wanted to find out the middle and then go on to the end. Stories seemed to make some sense of time, of history, of their lives. Stories were gifts from the gods enabling mortals to fashion the world in their own image. (Kearney, 2001, p. 5)

This method of ordering events to make sense and meaning appears to be crucial to the development and structure of human life. Story is not simply a literary category but an essential process of mind: without stories, we would be lost in a frightening and meaningless universe, drowning in a storm of fragments. We would also be more alone. Storytelling enables us to dramatize our lives as stories and to share these dramatized selves with each other. Kearney comments that:

> Every human experience is a life in search of a narrative. This is not simply because it strives to discover a pattern to cope with the experience of chaos and confusion. It is also because each human life is always already an implicit story. Our very finitude constitutes us as beings, who, to put it baldly, are born at the beginning and die at the end. (*ibid.*, p. 129)

But how can the writer develop a story? And how does story differ from **plot**? Imagine a court case reported in the local newspaper. A woman is sentenced to life imprisonment after being convicted of killing her husband's lover. These plain facts make up the plot: three characters; a terrible event; obvious motivation; a clear and just resolution. The outline of events is given to us by the newspaper report but, so far, we have no idea of the whole story, of how it all begin and what the steps were that led this woman to such a terrible act. The plot sets out the events in their sequential order, telling us *what* happened, but the story is much more concerned with *why* and *how*: character, motivation, place, circumstance and chance. To tell a story we need to imagine the small details of the characters' lives – the particular places they lived in, a city-centre loft or a scruffy backstreet terrace; the view from a bedroom window; the strange sounds the wife hears as she lies in bed sleepless and alone; how the husband behaved; what the lover looked like.

The key point is that the facts of the murder, as set out above, may be plain and clear, the eternal triangle plot so familiar in both life and fiction, yet there is no limit to the many ways that this story could be told. A complex psychological study, for example, of one or more of the protagonists; a crime thriller involving drug gangs; even science fiction – perhaps the three protagonists are on a spaceship. It could be told from the point of view of the husband, the lover or the wife. There may be another point of view – the detective who investigates the crime; someone who witnessed it: a child, perhaps, or a godlike omniscient narrator who sees all. And think of that moment when the idea of murder shifted from fantasy into possibility. Perhaps there was a particular trigger, something somebody said. The story could begin at the start of the affair, on the wedding day, the first night in prison, or at the discovery of the body. The events may unfold in a realistic narrative sequence or perhaps the story is pieced together through letters and diaries discovered years after the event by a grown-up grandchild. The form could be realistic or surreal: unfolding in a conventional step-by-step way or through **flashbacks** and fragmented jumpcuts. Each writer brings his or her own particular experience and viewpoint to events, real or imagined, and recounts them in a different way.

Writers sometimes get anxious about all those other writers before them who have bagged all the best plots. But if you extend your perspective and think back over the millennia of human existence, you might be comforted to realize that plots may be limited but that there are at least as many stories as there are human beings. It's the way you tell 'em.   *HL*

Writing ideas

Use the murder plot above. Write three opening paragraphs, each in the first person point of view of one of the characters. You can change the genders around if you wish. Begin each paragraph with the words: 'I never meant it to happen.' Which voice are you most drawn to? Imagine this character in detail: the way they dress, their tastes and interests. Avoid cliché and stereotype. Don't force a structure or pattern, let it emerge; try to feel into the character's emotions, to sink down into his or her body and mind. Let the events unfold in whatever time and order seems natural. Begin to live in the story.

Further reading

Kearney, Richard, *On Stories* (London: Routledge, 2001).

stream of consciousness

Attributed to both psychologist William James (Henry's older brother) and May Sinclair, a British novelist influenced by Freud, the concept indicates prose capturing the free flow of ideas. For prime examples, see Joyce's *Ulysses* (1922) and Woolf's *Mrs Dalloway* (1925), both presenting the interior life of their protagonists throughout the course of one day. While considered a modernist technique, it is now also espoused by contemporary writers, such as Irvine Welsh in *Trainspotting*, to capture a spoken first person interior narrative voice rather than an ordered written account. To produce some, simply write down everything that passes through your mind for a day: you'll soon realize that it is, in fact, a highly crafted device. So find a happy medium; write the tiny details and the tangents, but shape the work to maintain your reader's interest. *HN*

structure

As the word suggests, structure relates to the building blocks of a piece of writing, the way it all fits together and the complex relationship between each part. *The Hours* by Michael Cunningham, for example, is organized through parallel narratives, three women's stories which alternate, each chapter set in a different time and place, all three women connected in ways that reveal themselves as the novel unfolds. There are any number of ways that a narrative can be structured and if one arrangement isn't working, it may be helpful to find alternatives. Imagine yourself as an architect of fiction: does your story need a conventional three-bed semi, a modernist block of flats, or a tiny claustrophobic bedsit? *HL*

style

Proper words in proper places, according to Jonathan Swift. One of the most celebrated treatises on the subject is Strunk and White's *The Elements of Style*, which is available online, and amounts to 21 points including the following: write in a way that comes naturally; write with verbs and nouns; do not overwrite; avoid the use of qualifiers; do not explain too much; and avoid fancy words. 'The writer's style is himself', said Henry Green, and E. B. White (of Strunk and White) said, 'Style results more from what a person is than what he knows.' It's said that it takes a million words before you know how to write and somewhere in that effort your unique style is likely to emerge.

RG

Further reading

Strunk, William I. and E. B. White, *The Elements of Style* (New York: Allyn and Bacon, 1999); also available at www.bartleby.com/141.

subconscious, the

An area of mind of which the conscious is unaware, but which is available to it: a concept such as your address is not present at all times in your mind, but waits in the subconscious for recall. If it were in the unconscious, you'd never recall it, except in dreams and parapraxes.

Writers frequently play with what they want readers to know consciously and subconsciously. Narrative twists work best when readers feel that information has not been a total surprise, but is something they've already been given subconsciously: Ursula Le Guin's 'The Wife's Story' is a magnificent case in point.

HN

synopsis

A brief outline or summary of a work. You can write a synopsis *before* you begin writing, to help in thinking it through, or *after* you've written it, to use in seeking publication. Many agents and publishers initially insist on a synopsis plus sample chapters, rather than the whole work. The synopsis should give an overview of the story and, for a novel or script, a chapter-by-chapter or scene-by-scene summary. This is not the place to keep the agent or editor in suspense about who killed whom or whether the ending is happy, tragic or unresolved. It should include brief detail of characters and setting, as well as information about who the work is aimed at (adults/teenagers, etc.).

HL

syntax

The arrangement of words in a sentence – which matters. Here are a couple of suggestions which will improve your syntax.

It's a good idea to keep related words together. Positoning an adjective next to the noun it describes may be obvious, but, for example, placing a verb near its subject shows they are related. Placing a clause between subject and verb disrupts the natural order of the sentence. The second version of the sentence that follows is the more effective.

- *Bob Dylan, after an addled period in the '80s, produced some of his best work in the '90s.*
- *After an addled period in the '80s, Bob Dylan produced some of his best work in the '90s.*

Second, for maximum impact, place the words you wish to emphasize at the end of a sentence.

- Lost *is like* Twin Peaks *in the way it introduces layer upon layer of intrigue without offering much in the way of revelation.*
- *In the way it introduces layer upon layer of intrigue without offering much in the way of revelation,* Lost *is like* Twin Peaks.

What's the most important information in the sentence? The suggestion that *Lost* is like *Twin Peaks*. *RG*

television scripts

Television is a voraciously hungry consumer of scripts: everyday soap operas, small-screen films, sitcoms and serials are beamed into homes from hundreds of channels. From reruns of *Pride and Prejudice* to episodes of *Touched by an Angel*, you can always find something scripted for performance to watch at any time of day or night. This is great news for writers in that TV is a predatory medium, always desperately seeking new talent, and bad news in that often the shows screened are repeats of repeats, and the quality of writing is not necessarily as good as it could be.

The would-be writer for TV needs to know the industry and the medium inside out. The would-be writer also needs to get connected. What TV uses tomorrow it needs now, so moving in circles where you find out the latest information is always useful. There are courses out there which will introduce you to professionals (who cannot necessarily give you your entrance into the industry, but might give you up-to-date insider information as to what TV is looking for right now). The Arvon Foundation runs courses in screenwriting and TV Drama. Arvon courses are only five days long but they are intensive and, by the end of the week, you might know better whether this is a world you want to enter. University writing departments sometimes offer MAs in screenwriting, and these are worth considering for the tuition, the contacts and the exposure your work might gain: agents periodically trawl such departments for unsigned talent: no one, after all, wants to miss out on the next big thing.

In writing for television you will at some point write for shows you might ordinarily avoid watching. Don't sneer: never underestimate the skill; lots of writers cut their teeth writing for daytime soaps. By doing this, you'll demonstrate an ability to keep to strict deadlines, to produce the goods under pressure, to keep to the narrative brief and to write from nine till five regardless of whether you feel like writing or not. These skills are as vital as writing innovative narratives, fine characters and dazzling dialogue.

Finally, there is no substitute for looking at how the best in the industry go about it, so read as many scripts as you can. Look at formats and analyse the lengths of scenes and the way that good scriptwriters allow actors to help them develop characters. Look at the script work of Ricky Gervais, Andrew Davies, Jimmy McGovern, Peter Kay, Lynda La Plante, Stephen Poliakoff, and you'll see the masters at work.   *HN*

Further reading

The Arvon Foundation, www.arvonfoundation.org.

Gervais, Ricky and Steve Merchant, *The Office: The Scripts* (London: BBC Books, 2002).

Hobson, Dorothy, *Soap Opera* (Cambridge: Polity Press, 2002).

Smethurst, William, *Writing for Television: How to Write and Sell Successful TV Scripts* (Oxford: How To Books, 2005).

The Writers' Room, www.bbc.co.uk/writersroom.

Writing for Performance, www.robinkelly.btinternet.co.uk.

thesaurus

The classification of words and phrases according to a set of concepts and ideas. The original and best known, *Roget's Thesaurus*, first published in 1852 but kept up to date, with the most recent edition produced in 2006, is invaluable for writers, particularly when searching for synonyms. A thesaurus will enrich your vocabulary and will help you to write with skill and inventiveness, creative ingenuity, as well as fertile, ingenious, resourceful enthusiasm, although sometimes it could lead you to become romantic, high-flown, extravagant, grotesque, bizarre, fantastical and over-the-top. You can use online versions but they're not a patch on the printed book, which is great to browse, peruse, pore over, thumb, dip into . . .   *HL*

Further reading

Roget, Peter (ed. George Davidson), *Roget's Thesaurus of English Words and Phrases: 150th Anniversary Edition* (London: Penguin, 2006).

thought police

People, either real or imaginary, who inhabit your mind telling you what you should or shouldn't think. First used by George Orwell in his novel, *Nineteen Eighty-Four*, in which the Thinkpol were part of the totalitarian state structure. These days the term has proliferated to refer to any kind of thought control. There are special thought police for writers who tell you that you can't write if you're a mother; if you come from Wolverhampton; are under 30 or over 50; haven't got a dad called Amis; wear Lycra; are ugly; or haven't read *Ulysses*. Flush them out and shoot them down.   *HL*

(See **political correctness**)

Further reading
Orwell, George, *Nineteen Eighty-Four* (London: Penguin, 2004).

time

Time moves in one direction, so it seems: we begin at the beginning and work our way through to the end. Most of us have heard of Einstein's theory of relativity, even if only in *Doctor Who*, but we are so familiar with the sensation of time's forward movement that we take it as the universe's natural order. E. M. Forster famously described a story as 'a narrative of events arranged in a time sequence' (Forster, 1964, p. 37), which seems straightforward enough, until you consider that word: *arranged*. In fiction the writer is time lord.

The most familiar way of arranging the narrative is through a chronological sequence, describing events as they occur one after another: *Once upon a time Little Red Riding Hood set out to visit her grandmother. As she was going through the wood, she met with a wolf*. However, even within this straightforward structure there are ways of breaking up the time sequence. One of the most common is to pause the narrative while you insert expositional material: *Red Riding Hood had never met a wolf before. She had heard of wolves but . . .* or to **flashback** to an earlier time: *In the kitchen that morning, Mother had said, 'Red Riding Hood, take these cakes to your Grandmother, and be very careful when . . .'* These are useful techniques, adding texture and detail, but they need to be used carefully if the reader isn't to lose interest in the forward narrative or get lost, like *Star Trek*, in one too many time warps.

Narrative time order is the key to suspense. In the short story 'Solid Geometry', Ian McEwan's narrator drops just a few cryptic words in the first paragraph of an odd historical account, spoken in a dry, intellectual voice:

I believe my grandfather to have been a very fine diarist, and when I have finished editing the diaries and they are published I am certain he will receive the recognition due to him . . . I used to think that at the end of it all I would try, if it was possible, to divorce my wife Maisie, but now there is no need at all. (McEwan, 1997, p. 6)

Once that line, *now there is no need at all*, has lodged itself in your mind, you can't get rid of it; you just have to keep on reading the story until the very end when you find out what happened to Maisie (something extremely nasty and weird). In the meantime McEwan holds the reader in suspense, taking the reader with him as he explores the odd mind of the narrator.

Finding the most appropriate time arrangement for any piece of fiction is not just a clever trick for thriller writers but an essential element of structural form. One fine example is found in *Stuart: a Life Backwards* by Alexander Masters, the dramatized life story of a real person, described on the book cover as 'a chaotic, knife-wielding beggar'.

The time sequence of the book begins at the end of Stuart's life, and then chapter by chapter leads us back through time to Stuart's childhood and birth. This reversal works like memory, tracking down through the layers of a tragic life, seeking cause and meaning. It's worth noting that Masters had already written a first draft of the story in conventional order which wasn't working very well, when Stuart himself suggested that Masters rewrite it backwards, like a thriller, to make it more exciting. You may not discover the best way to organize time until the revision stage.

As well as the time *order* of events, the writer needs to make decisions about the time *span* of the narrative: will the story last for an hour, a day, for one year or a thousand? Some stories, like Virginia Woolf's *Mrs Dalloway*, last for just a single day. At the other extreme is Isaac Asimov's science fiction *Foundation* series which covers many millennia, swooping vertiginously through time on an epic scale.

E. M. Forster speaks of two kinds of life: 'life by the clock and the life of values' (Forster, 1964, p. 36). We are all familiar with 'life by the clock', but today we might translate 'life by values' as 'the inner life' or 'subjective time'. As we go about our business in the world, we experience a range of perceptions and shifts: the hours slip by when we're happy but even seconds can drag when we're bored. And in extreme moments something amazing happens: time slows down all around us, yet the mind moves and thinks at the same speed. At these times consciousness itself seems to expand, to become larger than our individual selves.

David Foster Wallace's story, 'Forever Overhead' catches just such an eternal moment, as a 13-year-old boy, terrified and exhilarated, climbs a long ladder to the top diving board:

Time slows. It thickens around you as your heart gets more and more beats out of each second. [. . .] No time is passing outside you at all. It is amazing. If you wanted you could really stay here forever, vibrating inside so fast you float motionless in time, like a bee over something sweet. (Foster Wallace, 1999, pp. 10–12)

Time is very strange and yet absolutely normal: as distant as the Big Bang and as close as breath. Inside the story, time tick-tocks along in its comforting way yet it also curves, loops and shifts. Modern physics has articulated the oddness of time but the fiction writer has always known it.   *HL*

Writing ideas
Read David Foster Wallace's story 'Forever Overhead'. Try to recall an event in your own experience when time altered its normal tick-tock rhythm – either slowing down or speeding up. Perhaps a moment of shock, fear, excitement or great happiness. Write a description of this experience using language and form that matches the experience. The aim is to try to recreate the sense of time-shift for the reader.

Further reading
Forster, E. M., *Aspects of the Novel* (London: Penguin, 1964).
McEwan, Ian, *First Love, Last Rites* (London: Vintage, 1997).
Wallace, David Foster, *Brief Interviews with Hideous Men* (London: Abacus, 1999).

title

What you call your piece of work. Apart from perhaps the cover, the title is the first thing the reader comes across and it may entice or repel, so what you call a piece of work is surprisingly important. Some titles are memorable and others not. One theory about what makes for a memorable title is that it should not be abstract, but something you can visualize. The title *On Beauty* creates no picture in the mind, but 'Blue Suede Shoes' does. However, it's easy to think of titles that conjure no image but still work – *Kiss Kiss, Bang Bang*, for instance. The relationship between title and work is important, too. The title has to in some way fit the work, has to feel at least appropriate and ideally inevitable. I've just read a novel called *The Speed of Light* and I have no idea why it has been called that. Another pitfall is the great title for a paltry work of art. Morrissey was once accused of coming up with wonderful titles but then forgetting to write the songs to go with them.

In terms of how you come up with a title, I suspect the norm is to write the work and then see if the title emerges organically from it. Often a title is a phrase found in the text. Sometimes a title will quote a well-known phrase from another text: *Far From The Madding Crowd* comes from Gray's 'Elegy Written in a Country Churchyard' and *Of Mice And Men* is from Robert Burns' 'To a Mouse'. Another popular approach to titles is to pun on an existing one – *To Grill A Mockingbird*, for example.

In the end, though, great book titles have a magic that is often impossible to explain. Look at *One Flew Over The Cuckoo's Nest.*   RG

transitions

'Passages that get a character from one place to another, or from one time to another' – Jack Bickham's definition (1994, p. 43). A transition, whether or not it involves a **section-break**, is used to show that the narrative has moved through time or space, or has omitted some irrelevant action. Transitions may be between one chapter and the next, one paragraph and another, one sentence and another, or within a sentence; but more often than not when we talk about transitions what we mean is the movement between one **scene** (or section) and another. Transitions are bridges, with feet on both sides of the divide.

Signalling the bridge, the connection between the end of one scene and the beginning of the succeeding one, can be a smart idea because it lets the reader know that the two sections or scenes are closely related. This way you can fight against losing or confusing your reader. The following passage from Suzannah Dunn's short story 'Slipping The Clutch' illustrates how that movement may be elegantly achieved.

> Before I could ask him how he knew which bookshop was my favourite, he smiled and disappeared. He *disappeared*, which he had never done before, to me. Or not that I had noticed. But perhaps, until then, I had been too happy to look behind me, or not for long enough, or far enough, or hard enough.
>
> The following week, I found him by *Languages*, scanning the shelves. (Dunn, 1999, p. 154)

The feet of the bridge here are marked on either side of the divide by bookshop references. The first section tells us that these characters are to meet in a bookshop. The second begins with signifiers that let us know we are in a bookshop ('*Languages*' and 'shelves'). The transition leaves a space between the two sections, but the bridge helps readers know that the new scene is connected to the last.

Transitions give readers a break, offer breathing space, and in that space they can rest from reading, and perhaps process the information that has gone before the break. The justification for using section-breaks and transitions is that it's preferable to cut your fiction up into sections which have some relation to the attention span of the human mind.   *RG*

Further reading

Bickham, Jack M., *Writing The Short Story: A Hands-On Guide for Creating Captivating Short Fiction* (Cincinnati: Writer's Digest Books, 1994).

Dunn, Suzannah, *Tenterhooks* (London: Flamingo, 1999).

unconscious, the

A part of the psyche said by Freud to contain repressed memories and ideas, and by Jung to comprise a personal unconscious developed by an individual through life experiences, and an inherited collective unconscious common to the human species. Jacques Lacan was profoundly influenced by Freud's notion of the unconscious, but for him, the unconscious refers to everything about a subject beyond the subject's conscious control: it is structured like language and *ça parle*: it speaks, that is to say illness and physical symptoms are corporeal metaphors for repressed unconscious desires. Let your unconscious speak to you in dreams: keep a dream diary. Play word association games: pick words out of books with pins, and write about the first things that come into your head when you find them.   *HN*

verbs

'Doing' or 'being' words. Verbs drive your sentences. Look at this extract from Raymond Carver's story 'Are These Actual Miles?'

> He goes for another drink. He adds ice and sees that his hand trembles. He holds the hand over the sink. He looks at the hand for a while, sets down the glass, and holds out the other hand. Then he picks up the glass and goes outside to sit on the steps. (Carver, in Oates, 1992, p. 585)

These few sentences are all motion – the verbs make them move. All action is achieved by verbs. Note here that each verb is out in the world working alone – no help from adverbs. A verb that hits the nail on the head first time – a verb that needs no qualification from an adverb – is a thing of beauty and a wonderful tool.

Active verbs communicate more directly and effectively than passive verbs. *The dog bit the cat* is a more efficient, less awkward sentence than *The cat was bitten by the dog.*   RG

villain

The main evil character in a story or drama; the antagonist set against the **hero** or **protagonist**; better known as The Baddie. Famous villains include The Queen of Hearts; Sauron; Lex Luthor; Darth Vader. Some heroes and villains become so inextricably locked in conflict that they are almost one person: Sherlock Holmes and Moriarty; Dr Frankenstein and the creature. Others, like Jekyll and Hyde and Bruce Banner and the Incredible Hulk are actually two people in the same body. The prototype of all villains is Satan, and his current loss of status in the West, along with that of his heroic protagonist, God, may explain why today's villains seem more psychologically flawed or badly brought up than purely evil. To be convincing, a contemporary villain needs motivation: we need to understand *why*.   HL

villanelle

The villanelle, described by Stephen Fry as requiring 'some of the qualities needed for suduko and crosswords', is one of the most fixed of **fixed forms**. It has five or more tercets (three-line stanzas) rhyming *aba* and a final quatrain (four-line stanza) rhyming *abaa*. The first and third lines of the opening stanza are repeated alternately as the third line of the subsequent stanza and then together as the final couplet of the poem. This creates a crafty patterning of words in which lines gain new meanings in juxtaposition with each other. The villanelle can be manipulated for humour or for serious effect, as in Dylan Thomas's 'Do not go gentle into that good night', one of the most famous.   HT

Further reading

Thomas, Dylan, *Poems* (London: Everyman/Phoenix, 1997).

voice

Readers and critics often note that a novelist has 'found' – or sometimes lost – her 'voice', meaning that attribute that makes an anonymous page of any of her novels immediately recognizable as hers, irrespective of narrator or point of view.

So what exactly is this mysterious quality? And how do you acquire it as a writer?

Like every aspect of the writer's skill, 'voice' can be boiled down to the arrangement of words on the page. The first step to finding yours is learning the basics of grammar and punctuation – even if only to subvert them. The second step is reading, and learning from what you read. This may, at first, feel more like losing your voice; but almost all great authors begin by 'trying on' the voice of earlier writers in whose fiction they are immersed. All emerge, paradoxically, with more robustly individual voices than if they had begun by trying to sound 'original'.

The third step towards finding your voice is identifying your subject. People, says Annie Dillard in *The Writing Life*, love pretty much the same things best, but a 'writer looking for subjects inquires not after what he loves best, but after what he alone loves at all' (Dillard, 1990, p. 67). Just as in everyday life people's voices grow louder when confident, writers' voices strengthen when they are true to their feelings about what they describe. This can demand courage. As Al Alvarez points out in *The Writer's Voice*, 'the authentic voice may not be the one you want to hear' (Alvarez, 2004, p. 29).

It may not parade your 'fine writing' or knowledge or education. It may be more dissident, or come alive on less impressive or 'acceptable' topics. But this is the voice that will, Alvarez says, sound unlike any other, speaking directly to your reader, right in their ear, and in its own distinctive way. This is 'the vehicle by which a writer expresses his aliveness' (Alvarez, 2004, p. 15).

Even though it is usually close to the writer's everyday speaking voice, this authentic, distinctive note is not always heard in a first draft, or in the white heat of inspiration. The urgent, raw and demotic can be the product of careful revision. Toni Morrison, for instance, says that when she does a first draft, it's usually flawed by her tendency to write in the language of everyday speech, which is the language of business, media, the language we use to get through the day. Later she has to 'rewrite, discard, and remove the print-quality of language to put back the oral quality, where intonation, volume and gesture are all there' (Morrison, in Tate (ed.), 1983).

When a writer has found his own voice, Alvarez says, 'it picks the locks, opens the doors, and enables him to begin to say what he wants to say' (Alvarez, 2004, p. 20). And this, for the writer, is the ultimate and possibly the only test of any book he or she writes.   *JN*

Further reading

Alvarez, Al, *The Writer's Voice* (New York: W.W. Norton & Co., 2004).

Dillard, Anne, *The Writing Life* (New York: Harper Perennial, 1990).

Tate, Claudia (ed.), *Black Women Writers at Work* (New York: Continuum, 1983), p. 126.

weather

These days few of us work on the land, and most of us watch the skies for no more than a chance to sunbathe, or to see if the match is going to be rained off. Yet the weather still colours our emotional landscape: we talk about being in a fog, or at sea, or in a storm of tears. And it still shapes our increasingly urban and secular fiction, functioning as a modern-day Jacob's ladder, the site of encounters with the freakish, the uncontrollable and the unsafe, with that which lies beyond our everyday concerns.

In *Enduring Love*, Ian McEwan's opening chapter depends as dramatically on the weather as any by Thomas Hardy. The narrator, Joe, and his wife have chosen a picnic site 'partly protected from a strong, gusty wind' when they notice a balloon with a terrified boy in the basket. Soon five men, including Joe, are clinging to its ropes:

> A mighty fist socked the balloon in two rapid blows, one-two, the second more vicious than the first. And the first was vicious . . . Into our amazed silence, before the shouting could resume, the second punch came and knocked the balloon up and westwards. (McEwan, 1998, p. 13)

McEwan uses the wind to put his characters under pressure: 'Suddenly we were treading the air with all our weight in the grip of our fists' (p. 13). The decisions they take about whether or not to hang on reveal them for what they are. Unexpected conflicts and connections spring out of their seemingly random encounter caused by the wind.

McEwan's weather shapes his plot: Joe's life is going to change. But weather can also be used to illuminate character: a fictional woman staring out at the rain is probably feeling gloomy. Descriptions of weather can also be metaphorical, slowing the pace and directing our attention inward, as in this passage from Michèle Roberts' *The Mistressclass*, where Adam reaches psychological meltdown:

Adam felt as if he were very ancient, made of stone, a stone man left outside all winter long, streaks of moss greening his shoulders, the rain beating against his back . . . He was scoured white by the weather. His nose was eroded, his fingertips, his toes. A stone man couldn't do what was required of husbands. Talk. Sort things out. He could only bend down and fill his mouth with earth. (Roberts, 2003, p. 201)

The most inveterate townie will understand this language of park and garden. Yet Adam has become an emblem of ancient suffering. Like Virginia Woolf in Section II of *To the Lighthouse*, Roberts uses weather to convey the passage of time: people have often felt like this; Adam's misery is long-standing. Also, both he and Joe enter an unaccustomed space. For Joe, this space is moral: he must ponder his decision to let go of the rope. For Adam, it is psychological: his damaged spirit needs succour. Through their descriptions of the weather, both authors push their crisis-ridden characters into a zone where normal rules do not apply. You can, too.   *JN*

Further reading
McEwan, Ian, *Enduring Love* (London: Vintage, 1998).
Roberts, Michèle, *The Mistressclass* (London: Virago, 2003).

white space
The space around the text may be used to make the page inviting to the reader. To most readers, a page which has been broken into paragraphs and includes some dialogue is more accessible than a solid rectangle of text. From the late twentieth century onwards there has been a tendency for writers to leave more white space on the page. Apart from the use of paragraphs and dialogue, this may come from **section-breaks**. In this same period, the shorter paragraph has become more popular, a further contributing factor to the increased use of white space in prose writing.   *RG*

work
The workplace is where many of us spend most of our waking hours. It is where we earn our living, fulfil ourselves, grow bored, make enemies and friends, and often meet our life partners. Few things express a person's temperament and class as vividly as her choice, or lack of choice, or even lack, of a job. In *Bleak House*, for example, Charles Dickens never needs to say that Richard Carstone is unstable: he simply shows him unable to settle on a

career, just as he lets us see Harold Skimpole sponging, and Inspector Bucket living for his job. Their ways of life divide them from Sir Leicester Dedlock, who does not need to work or sponge, as much as from the poverty-stricken Jo, who sweeps the streets to survive.

Work can provide the challenge that brings your characters to life, giving them the chance to pit their wits against an opponent, a rival corporation, their bosses – or just themselves. Here is Kip, the Sikh soldier, disabling a mine in Michael Ondaatje's *The English Patient*:

> Six black wires . . . One could of course make a red wire negative. But this opponent had not just concreted the thing but painted all the characters black. Kip was being pulled into a psychological vortex. With the knife he began to scrape the paint free, revealing a red, a blue, a green. Would his opponent have switched them? He'd have to set up a detour with black wire of his own like an oxbow river and then test the loop for positive or negative power. Then he would check it for fading power and know where the danger lay. (Ondaatje, 1992, p. 99)

By allowing Kip no choice but to risk his life and that of his lover, Ondaatje not only gives us a snapshot of a war, but he also dramatizes the sapper's aloof and committed nature, and shows us, through convincing use of technical detail, how it is, in Shakespeare's words in Sonnet 111, 'subdued to what it works in'.

But your characters' jobs need not be matters of life and death, or depend on expert research. For instance, in Madeleine Bourdouxhe's *Marie*, the eponymous heroine likes housework, including the weight of the coal buckets she carries up from the cellar into her home. Her 'hands plunge into dead fires or into soapy water, they rub the rust off a piece of metal and grease it, spread polish, and, after a meal, sweep the scraps from a table in one great circular movement' (Bourdouxhe, 1998, pp. 56–7). Like Ondaatje's 'scrape' and 'test', Bourdouxhe's verbs – 'lunge', 'rub' and 'sweep' – are energetic, precise, and bring both activity and character to life. She draws not on specialist knowledge, but on the same observation and sensuous pleasure in the everyday which characterizes her heroine as effectively as Ondaatje portrays Kip.

Whether researched, invented or observed, a zestful approach to work's potential in fiction will animate your prose, and mean that you need not resort to creating a central character who is a student or writer.   *JN*

Further reading

Bourdouxhe, Madeleine, *Marie* (London: Bloomsbury, 1998).

Ondaatje, Michael, *The English Patient* (London: Bloomsbury, 1992).

workshops

Writing can be a lonely business. There aren't many places where it's possible to talk about how to pace a scene or restructure an over-complex plot. Normal folk don't really care *how* books are written; they just want to read them, so the best people to talk to about writing are other writers. Don't believe the snobbish myths about 'real authors' not needing workshops or groups. Most writers have always had some kind of support and interaction with others: literary biographies and letters describe countless meetings, friendships and collaborations. Past and present writers, famous, unknown, published and unpublished, meet and have always met in informal networks. Workshops and courses are the modern-day equivalent of the fashionable literary network: open to all, not just the fortunate few who know the password.

The major value of a writers' workshop is to have your work read and discussed by the other members of the group. The need to get something written by a particular date and time is a powerful motivator: very few of us work hard unless we have to, so the workshop deadline is the writer's friend. Another benefit is that you can read other people's drafts. You can learn a great deal by seeing a story, script or poem in the process of making. Close reading of others' work can help you to see your own more clearly, as well as giving you a number of useful analytical and creative tools to work with.

As well as motivation and editing experience, workshops give you *permission* to be a writer. It is a humbling but powerful experience to hear your half-formed pages being given as much attention and respect as if they were already an actual story or screenplay. Stephen King comments in *On Writing* that the main benefit of writing courses and groups is that they take writing seriously; 'for aspiring writers who have been looked upon with pitying condescension by their friends and relatives . . . this is a wonderful thing' (King, 2000, p. 283).

The word *workshop* has its roots in a manufacturing context, bringing to mind engineering tool rooms, steel foundries, motor maintenance depots, etc. These practical and pragmatic connotations are useful pointers to the elements that make up an effective writers' workshop. First, it needs to be productive: everybody in the group should regularly write and present work to be discussed and also give careful attention to other people's work. Too much informal chatting, even chat about writing, can become a substitute for the actual writing itself. Second, the workshop needs to have a relaxed but definite structure in which people get a planned and equal amount of time. It's best to agree a timetable in advance and set deadlines for how work should be disseminated to group members. Reading aloud takes a lot of time but it can give a much better insight into how the writer intends the work to be understood. However, if drafts are distributed and read in advance, you get more considered feedback. You takes your choice.

It's helpful if the writer whose work is being discussed keeps quiet and simply listens while the group talks about his or her work. This method models the usual relationship between published writers and readers and reinforces the experience of *writing as a process*. It can be frustrating, particularly when people misinterpret a character's intentions or miss the whole point of a story. The temptation is to leap in and put them right, but this should be resisted. The main value of keeping quiet is that you actually *hear what is being said* rather than the sound of your own indignant counter-arguments or embarrassed self-justifications. The aim is for a group discussion of the work, rather than a series of reader/writer dialogues. To balance this, people discussing the work should try to avoid directing remarks and questions at the writer while the discussion is going on, adopting a more objective language, commenting on the writing itself. This may seem contrived and silly at first, but once established it works well and people soon get used to it: in fact you may find that it's a positive relief to have the attention focused on the work while you eavesdrop on the reader's experience.

There can be problems in workshops: people can be brutal in their criticism, bruising the confidence of others. On the other hand, praise in workshops is motivating but too much of it can become addictive. We wouldn't be human if we didn't need praise but workshops should be places where work in progress is looked at honestly and realistically, with readers trying to respond as clearly and truthfully as they can. This sounds easy but it isn't. Much more common is vague, unfocused feedback: *I really liked it*; *There's too much description*. Focusing on the work rather than the person helps, but it may also be useful to have an agreed process for discussing a piece, looking at particular aspects in order. For example: *big stuff*: themes, story, plot, genre, form, structure; *middle-sized stuff*: character, setting, point of view, voice, pace; *small stuff*: vocabulary, sentence structure, imagery.

Punctuation and spelling comes last. On a course, the class tutor or workshop leader could establish and maintain guidelines, reminding people that the point of the workshop is to find the work's best potential, and they might also draw out discussion of elements that haven't been covered.

Finally, it's worth remembering that a workshop is not an English Literature seminar: group members are not operating as literary critics but as writers and readers. In the writers' workshop, as in the engineering toolroom, it's the art, craft and mechanics of *making* that matter.   *HL*

Further reading
Gardner, John, *On Becoming a Novelist* (London: Norton, 1999).
King, Stephen, *On Writing* (London: Hodder and Stoughton, 2000).

writing practice
Anaïs Nin suggests that writers need to keep in training: 'Writing . . . as one practises the piano every day keeps one nimble, and then when the great moments of inspiration come, one is in good form, supple and smooth' (Newman et al., 2004, p. 10). Natalie Goldburg came up with the term 'Writing Practice' for this, and has suggested a set of guidelines, her 'Rules of Writing Practice':

1. Keep your hand moving
2. Lose control
3. Be specific
4. Don't think
5. Worry about punctuation and grammar later
6. You are free to write the worst junk
7. Go for the jugular. (Goldburg, 1991, pp. 1–4)

One reason to develop this discipline is that it keeps us writing-fit in the same way that a tennis player might be match-fit. Another is that put forward by Dorothea Brande in *Becoming A Writer*: she suggests that writing each day will develop the habit of opening up a channel to the unconscious mind. *RG*

Further reading
Brande, Dorothea, *Becoming a Writer* (New York: Harcourt Brace & Company, 1934).
Goldburg, Natalie, *Wild Mind* (London: Rider, 1991).

zeitgeist

Literally 'the spirit of the time', a term meaning everything that's new, fashionable, in the groove. Writers sometimes believe that if they follow the
literary mood of the time – gangster scripts, chick-lit, multicultural sagas –
they'll inevitably be more successful. The trouble is that the zeitgeist is usually
one step beyond and we rarely know what it is until it's gone past us. But
rational consciousness, *knowing*, is not all that we need. Writers who are in
touch with their time and who write with commitment and passion are *part*
of the zeitgeist; one of the makers and shakers, not one of the followers.

HL

Further Reading

Allott, Miriam, *Novelists on the Novel* (London: Routledge and Kegan Paul, 1965).

Anderson, Linda, *Creative Writing: A Workbook with Readings* (London: Routledge, 2005).

Bell, Julia and Paul Magrs (eds), *The Creative Writing Coursebook* (London: Macmillan, 2001).

Bickham, Jack M., *Writing the Short Story: A Hands-On Guide for Creating Captivating Short Fiction* (Cincinnati: Writer's Digest Books, 1994).

Booker, Christopher, *The Seven Basic Plots: Why We Tell Stories* (London: Continuum, 2004).

Boylan, Clare (ed.), *The Agony and The Ego* (London: Penguin, 1993).

Brande, Dorothea, *Becoming a Writer* (1934) (London: Pan, 1996).

Burroway, Janet, *Writing Fiction: A Guide To Narrative Craft* (Sixth Edition, New York: Longman, 2003).

Charters, Ann, *The Story and Its Writer: An Introduction to Short Fiction* (New York: St Martin's Press, 1995).

Crystal, David, *The Cambridge Encyclopedia of The English Language* (Second Edition, Cambridge: Cambridge University Press, 2003).

Dorner, Jane, *The Internet: A Writer's Guide* (London: A&C Black, 2000).

Frey, James N., *How To Write A Damn Good Novel* (London: Macmillan, 1988).

Friedman, Bonnie, *Writing Past Dark* (New York: HarperCollins, 1994).

Fry, Stephen, *The Ode Less Travelled: Unlocking the Poet Within* (London: Hutchinson Books, 2005).

Gardner, John, *On Becoming a Novelist* (London: Norton, 1999).

Goldberg, Natalie, *Wild Mind: Living the Writer's Life* (London: Rider, 1991).

Goldman, William, *Adventures in the Screen Trade* (London: Abacus, 1996).

Graham, Robert, Helen Newall, Heather Leach and John Singleton (eds), *The Road To Somewhere: A Creative Writing Companion* (Basingstoke: Palgrave, 2005).

Graham, Robert, *How To Write Fiction (And Think About It)* (Basingstoke: Palgrave, 2006).

Grenville, Kate, *The Writing Book* (St Leonards, NSW: Allen & Unwin, 1998).

Hatcher, Jeffrey, *The Art and Craft of Playwriting* (Cincinnati: Writers' Digest Books, 2000).

Herbert, W. N. and Matthew Hollis (eds), *Strong Words: Modern Poets on Modern Poetry* (Northumberland: Bloodaxe Books, 2000).

Hobsbaum, Philip, *Metre, Rhythm and Verse Form* (London: Routledge, 1996).

King, Stephen, *On Writing* (London: Hodder and Stoughton, 2000).

Lamott, Anne, *Bird By Bird – Some Instructions on Writing and Life* (New York: Anchor Books, 1995).

Further Reading

Leader, Zachery, *Writer's Block* (Baltimore: Johns Hopkins University Press, 1991).

Lodge, David, *The Art of Fiction* (London: Penguin, 1992).

McGrath, Declan, *Screenwriting* (Hove: RotoVision, 2003).

McKee, Robert, *Story: Substance, Structure and Style and the Principles of Screenwriting* (London: Methuen, 1999).

Newman, Jenny, Edmund Cusick and Aileen La Tourette (eds), *The Writer's Workbook* (London: Arnold, 2004).

Plimpton, George, *The Writer's Chapbook* (New York: Penguin, 1992).

Sharples, Mike, *How We Write* (London: Routledge, 1999).

Smethurst, William, *Writing for Television: How to Write and Sell Successful TV Scripts* (Oxford: How To Books, 2005).

Smith, Hazel, *The Writing Experiment: Strategies for Innovative Creative Writing* (St Leonards, NSW: Allen & Unwin, 2005).

Strunk, William I. and E. B. White, *The Elements of Style* (New York: Allyn and Bacon, 1999). Or available online: www.bartleby.com/141.

Sweeney, Matthew and J. H. Williams, *Writing Poetry: and Getting Published* (London: Hodder Headline, 1997).

Taylor, Val, *Stage Writing: A Practical Guide* (Ramsbury: Crowood Press, 2002).

Timpane, John and Maureen Watts, *Poetry for Dummies* (New York: For Dummies, 2001).

Truss, Lynne, *Eats, Shoots & Leaves* (London: Profile, 2005).

Turner, Barry (ed.), *The Writer's Handbook* (London: Macmillan, published annually).

Vogel, Christopher, *The Writer's Journey* (London: Pan, 1999).

Whitworth, John, *Writing Poetry* (London: A&C Black, 2001).

Woolf, Virginia, *A Room of One's Own* (London: Penguin Modern Classics, 2003).

Useful websites

www.artscouncil.org.uk

www.arvonfoundation.org

www.bbc.co.uk/writersroom

http://books.guardian.co.uk/shortshortstories

www.blogger.com

www.contemporarywriters.com

www.ebooks.com

www.jondorf.com/youngplaywrights.html

www.mslexia.co.uk

www.modernhaiku.org

www.nawe.co.uk

http://poemsthatgo.com

www.poetryslam.com

http://en.wikipedia.org/wiki/African_American_literature

www.abc.net.au/arts/stuff-art/stuff-art99/stuff98/wordstuf/index.htm

www.writeoutloud.net

www.writernet.co.uk

www.writersdigest.com/101sites/2003_index.asp

www.writersservices.com

Alternative Routes

The lists below are organized into related categories enabling you to take alternative routes through this book. They can be used by individuals who wish to explore a particular topic, or by tutors planning a lesson or longer programme of study around a specific theme.

Attitudes
age
ageism
caricature
class
dialect
gender
political correctness
race
sexuality
stereotype
thought police

Beginning
beginning
creative process
creativity
daydreaming
desk
displacement activities
dreams
eavesdropping
experience
gestation
imagination
influence
intentions
journals

journey
language
notebooks
observation
pictures
planning
play
reading
research
skills
title
voice
workshops
writing practice
zeitgeist

Blocks
block
chaos
clutter
creativity
displacement activities
envy
failure
flailing and *kvetching*
rejection
thought police

Characters, narrators and viewpoints
caricature
character
dialect
hero
heroine
monologue
multiple viewpoint
names
narrator
omniscient narrator
point of view
protagonist
single viewpoint
stereotype
villain

Design and layout
double-spacing
fonts
house style
length
page design
paragraphs
punctuation

section-breaks
spellcheck
white space

Editing and revision
abstract
anachronism
archaisms
clichés
clutter
concrete
drafts
editing
feedback
grammar
proofreading
punctuation
revision
spellcheck
structure
workshops

Experimental writing
automatic writing
creativity
digression
experimental poetry

193

experimental writing
found poetry
imagination
IT
magic realism
metafiction
modernism
play
postmodernism
stream of con-sciousness

Fiction
action
anachronism
breathing space
change
character
climax
conflict
craft
description
detail
dialogue
digression
directness
drama
dramatization
emotion
endings
exposition
fiction
flashback
hero
heroine
hooks
image
immediacy
in medias res
inciting incident
love
middle

multiple viewpoint
narrative
narrative tension
narrator
novel
omniscient narrator
pace
pictures
plant and pay-off
plot
point of view
premise
protagonist
quest plot
quilting
romance plot
scenes
setting
sex
short story
simple linear plot
single viewpoint
story
structure
time
title
transitions
villain
voice
weather

Form and genre
autobiography
children, writing for
crime
drama
genre
graphic novel
magic realism
metafiction

monologue
novel
poetry
radio
scriptwriting
short story
story
television scripts

Grammar and punctuation
abstract
adjective
adverb
alliteration and assonance
apostrophe
concrete
grammar
metaphor
noun
punctuation
sentence
simile
syntax
verbs

Ideas and movements
Death of the Author
modernism
postmodernism
Romanticism

IT
Amazon
blank screen
blogs
e-books
email
experimental poetry

experimental writing
IT
publishing
software
spellcheck
zeitgeist

Plot
hero
heroine
journey
love
narrative
philosophy of composition
plot
premise
protagonist
quest plot
realism
romance plot
sex
simple linear plot
villain

Poetry
alliteration and assonance
archaisms
ballad
epic
experimental poetry
fixed forms
found poetry
haiku
imagery
lineation
lyric
metaphor
metre and rhythm
phonemic pattern

poetic genre
poetry
poetry reading
   and perform-
   ance
prose poetry
repetition
rhyme
sonnet
villanelle

Publishing
advance
agent
bestsellers
editor
manuscript
money
plagiarism
proofreading
publishing
rejection
self-publishing
synopsis

Reading and research
Amazon
bookshops
data
detail
e-books
English
graphic novels
index cards
intentions
IT
journals
language
learning

library
non-fiction
notebooks
reader(s)
reading
research
thesaurus

Scriptwriting
dialogue
drama
dramatization
monologue
radio
scenes
scriptwriting
software
television scripts

Self, mind and consciousness
autobiography
automatic writing
being a writer
consciousness
creativity
daydreaming
Death of the
   Author
dreams
genius
gestation
memory
play
stream of con-
   sciousness
subconscious, the
thought police
time
unconscious, the

Skills
being a writer
craft
creativity
daydreaming
dreams
eavesdropping
English
experience
failure
genius
imagination
imagery
influences
language
learning
love
memory
observation
play
reading
reflective writing
rejection
research
skills
style
voice

Structure
chapters
climax
conflict
craft
digression
endings
epistolary
flashback
hooks
immediacy
inciting incident

length
middle
pace
pattern
plant and pay-off
quest plot
quilting
scenes
setting
simple linear plot
structure
time
transitions

Workshops and groups
feedback
learning
poetry readings
   and perform-
   ances
reader(s)
reflective writing
rejection
zeitgeist

Writing life
being a writer
desk
eavesdropping
garrets
genius
gestation
journey
learning
notebooks
room
skills
zeitgeist